The Author

Edward de Vere, 17th Earl of Oxford

Biography and Bibliography
After the Play

The Merchant of Venice

By Edward de Vere

Art:
Portrait of Edward de Vere
17th Earl of Oxford (1550-1604)

This edition produced by
Verus Publishing

V | P

www.verusbooks.com

ISBN: 978-1-951267-34-6
Imprint / Publisher: Verus Publishing

A Preverse

Drone on ye learned scholars of the day
As to with whom the words ahead the credit lay.
For our part though can be no further doubt
That the author of these words has been found out
To be a person lordly and refined
On whom the light of wit so boldly shined
That to keep this wit from tearing in the fray
He gave another, lesser wit his say.

Now let the least of wits
That writes these paltry lines
Yield to him whose peerless name
Should be with reverence spake.
Let this name be not of history's misassigns
Whose pen and verse have made the earth to shake.

The Merchant of Venice

By Edward de Vere

The Main Characters

Antonio – A prominent merchant in Venice

Bassanio – Good friend of Antonio.

Gratiano – A friend of Antonio and Bassanio.

Lorenzo – Also a friend of Antonio and Bassanio.

Portia – A rich heiress.

Nerissa – Portia's waiting maid.

Balthazar & Stephano – Servants of Portia.

Shylock – A Jewish moneylender & father of Jessica

Jessica – The daughter of Shylock.

Tubal – A friend of Shylock.

Launcelot Gobbo – A servant of Shylock.

Old Gobbo – The blind father of Launcelot.

Leonardo – The slave of Bassanio.

Duke of Venice – The authority who presides over the case of Shylock's bond.

Prince of Morocco & Prince of Aragon – Two suitors to Portia.

Salarino and Salanio – friends of Antonio and Bassanio.

Salerio – a messenger from Venice.

And now, the Play...

ACT I

SCENE I.

Venice. A street.

Enter ANTONIO, SALARINO, and SALANIO

ANTONIO

    In sooth, I know not why I am so sad:
    It wearies me; you say it wearies you;
    But how I caught it, found it, or came by it,
    What stuff 'tis made of, whereof it is born,
    I am to learn;
    And such a want-wit sadness makes of me,
    That I have much ado to know myself.

SALARINO

    Your mind is tossing on the ocean;
    There, where your argosies with portly sail,
    Like signiors and rich burghers on the flood,
    Or, as it were, the pageants of the sea,
    Do overpeer the petty traffickers,
    That curtsy to them, do them reverence,
    As they fly by them with their woven wings.

SALANIO

    Believe me, sir, had I such venture forth,
    The better part of my affections would
    Be with my hopes abroad. I should be still
    Plucking the grass, to know where sits the wind,
    Peering in maps for ports and piers and roads;
    And every object that might make me fear
    Misfortune to my ventures, out of doubt
    Would make me sad.

SALARINO

    My wind cooling my broth

Would blow me to an ague, when I thought
What harm a wind too great at sea might do.
I should not see the sandy hour-glass run,
But I should think of shallows and of flats,
And see my wealthy Andrew dock'd in sand,
Vailing her high-top lower than her ribs
To kiss her burial. Should I go to church
And see the holy edifice of stone,
And not bethink me straight of dangerous rocks,
Which touching but my gentle vessel's side,
Would scatter all her spices on the stream,
Enrobe the roaring waters with my silks,
And, in a word, but even now worth this,
And now worth nothing? Shall I have the thought
To think on this, and shall I lack the thought
That such a thing bechanced would make me sad?
But tell not me; I know, Antonio
Is sad to think upon his merchandise.

ANTONIO
Believe me, no: I thank my fortune for it,
My ventures are not in one bottom trusted,
Nor to one place; nor is my whole estate
Upon the fortune of this present year:
Therefore my merchandise makes me not sad.

SALARINO
Why, then you are in love.

ANTONIO
Fie, fie!

SALARINO
Not in love neither? Then let us say you are sad,
Because you are not merry: and 'twere as easy
For you to laugh and leap and say you are merry,
Because you are not sad. Now, by two-headed Janus,
Nature hath framed strange fellows in her time:

Some that will evermore peep through their eyes
And laugh like parrots at a bag-piper,
And other of such vinegar aspect
That they'll not show their teeth in way of smile,
Though Nestor swear the jest be laughable.

Enter BASSANIO, LORENZO, and GRATIANO

SALANIO
Here comes Bassanio, your most noble kinsman,
Gratiano and Lorenzo. Fare ye well:
We leave you now with better company.
SALARINO
I would have stay'd till I had made you merry,
If worthier friends had not prevented me.
ANTONIO
Your worth is very dear in my regard.
I take it, your own business calls on you
And you embrace the occasion to depart.
SALARINO
Good morrow, my good lords.
BASSANIO
Good signiors both, when shall we laugh? say, when?
You grow exceeding strange: must it be so?
SALARINO
We'll make our leisures to attend on yours.

Exeunt Salarino and Salanio

LORENZO
My Lord Bassanio, since you have found Antonio,
We two will leave you: but at dinner-time,
I pray you, have in mind where we must meet.
BASSANIO
I will not fail you.

GRATIANO
> You look not well, Signior Antonio;
> You have too much respect upon the world:
> They lose it that do buy it with much care:
> Believe me, you are marvellously changed.

ANTONIO
> I hold the world but as the world, Gratiano;
> A stage where every man must play a part,
> And mine a sad one.

GRATIANO
> Let me play the fool:
> With mirth and laughter let old wrinkles come,
> And let my liver rather heat with wine
> Than my heart cool with mortifying groans.
> Why should a man, whose blood is warm within,
> Sit like his grandsire cut in alabaster?
> Sleep when he wakes and creep into the jaundice
> By being peevish? I tell thee what, Antonio--
> I love thee, and it is my love that speaks--
> There are a sort of men whose visages
> Do cream and mantle like a standing pond,
> And do a wilful stillness entertain,
> With purpose to be dress'd in an opinion
> Of wisdom, gravity, profound conceit,
> As who should say 'I am Sir Oracle,
> And when I ope my lips let no dog bark!'
> O my Antonio, I do know of these
> That therefore only are reputed wise
> For saying nothing; when, I am very sure,
> If they should speak, would almost damn those ears,
> Which, hearing them, would call their brothers fools.
> I'll tell thee more of this another time:
> But fish not, with this melancholy bait,
> For this fool gudgeon, this opinion.

Come, good Lorenzo. Fare ye well awhile:
I'll end my exhortation after dinner.

LORENZO

Well, we will leave you then till dinner-time:
I must be one of these same dumb wise men,
For Gratiano never lets me speak.

GRATIANO

Well, keep me company but two years moe,
Thou shalt not know the sound of thine own tongue.

ANTONIO

Farewell: I'll grow a talker for this gear.

GRATIANO

Thanks, i' faith, for silence is only commendable
In a neat's tongue dried and a maid not vendible.

Exeunt GRATIANO and LORENZO

ANTONIO

Is that any thing now?

BASSANIO

Gratiano speaks an infinite deal of nothing, more
than any man in all Venice. His reasons are as two
grains of wheat hid in two bushels of chaff: you
shall seek all day ere you find them, and when you
have them, they are not worth the search.

ANTONIO

Well, tell me now what lady is the same
To whom you swore a secret pilgrimage,
That you to-day promised to tell me of?

BASSANIO

'Tis not unknown to you, Antonio,
How much I have disabled mine estate,
By something showing a more swelling port
Than my faint means would grant continuance:
Nor do I now make moan to be abridged

From such a noble rate; but my chief care
Is to come fairly off from the great debts
Wherein my time something too prodigal
Hath left me gaged. To you, Antonio,
I owe the most, in money and in love,
And from your love I have a warranty
To unburden all my plots and purposes
How to get clear of all the debts I owe.

ANTONIO

I pray you, good Bassanio, let me know it;
And if it stand, as you yourself still do,
Within the eye of honour, be assured,
My purse, my person, my extremest means,
Lie all unlock'd to your occasions.

BASSANIO

In my school-days, when I had lost one shaft,
I shot his fellow of the self-same flight
The self-same way with more advised watch,
To find the other forth, and by adventuring both
I oft found both: I urge this childhood proof,
Because what follows is pure innocence.
I owe you much, and, like a wilful youth,
That which I owe is lost; but if you please
To shoot another arrow that self way
Which you did shoot the first, I do not doubt,
As I will watch the aim, or to find both
Or bring your latter hazard back again
And thankfully rest debtor for the first.

ANTONIO

You know me well, and herein spend but time
To wind about my love with circumstance;
And out of doubt you do me now more wrong
In making question of my uttermost
Than if you had made waste of all I have:

Then do but say to me what I should do
That in your knowledge may by me be done,
And I am prest unto it: therefore, speak.
BASSANIO
In Belmont is a lady richly left;
And she is fair, and, fairer than that word,
Of wondrous virtues: sometimes from her eyes
I did receive fair speechless messages:
Her name is Portia, nothing undervalued
To Cato's daughter, Brutus' Portia:
Nor is the wide world ignorant of her worth,
For the four winds blow in from every coast
Renowned suitors, and her sunny locks
Hang on her temples like a golden fleece;
Which makes her seat of Belmont Colchos' strand,
And many Jasons come in quest of her.
O my Antonio, had I but the means
To hold a rival place with one of them,
I have a mind presages me such thrift,
That I should questionless be fortunate!
ANTONIO
Thou know'st that all my fortunes are at sea;
Neither have I money nor commodity
To raise a present sum: therefore go forth;
Try what my credit can in Venice do:
That shall be rack'd, even to the uttermost,
To furnish thee to Belmont, to fair Portia.
Go, presently inquire, and so will I,
Where money is, and I no question make
To have it of my trust or for my sake.

Exeunt

SCENE II:

Belmont. A room in PORTIA'S house.

Enter PORTIA and NERISSA

PORTIA

By my troth, Nerissa, my little body is aweary of
this great world.

NERISSA

You would be, sweet madam, if your miseries were in
the same abundance as your good fortunes are: and
yet, for aught I see, they are as sick that surfeit
with too much as they that starve with nothing. It
is no mean happiness therefore, to be seated in the
mean: superfluity comes sooner by white hairs, but
competency lives longer.

PORTIA

Good sentences and well pronounced.

NERISSA

They would be better, if well followed.

PORTIA

If to do were as easy as to know what were good to
do, chapels had been churches and poor men's
cottages princes' palaces. It is a good divine that
follows his own instructions: I can easier teach
twenty what were good to be done, than be one of the
twenty to follow mine own teaching. The brain may
devise laws for the blood, but a hot temper leaps
o'er a cold decree: such a hare is madness the
youth, to skip o'er the meshes of good counsel the
cripple. But this reasoning is not in the fashion to
choose me a husband. O me, the word 'choose!' I may
neither choose whom I would nor refuse whom I
dislike; so is the will of a living daughter curbed

by the will of a dead father. Is it not hard,
Nerissa, that I cannot choose one nor refuse none?

NERISSA

Your father was ever virtuous; and holy men at their
death have good inspirations: therefore the lottery,
that he hath devised in these three chests of gold,
silver and lead, whereof who chooses his meaning
chooses you, will, no doubt, never be chosen by any
rightly but one who shall rightly love. But what
warmth is there in your affection towards any of
these princely suitors that are already come?

PORTIA

I pray thee, over-name them; and as thou namest
them, I will describe them; and, according to my
description, level at my affection.

NERISSA

First, there is the Neapolitan prince.

PORTIA

Ay, that's a colt indeed, for he doth nothing but
talk of his horse; and he makes it a great
appropriation to his own good parts, that he can
shoe him himself. I am much afeard my lady his
mother played false with a smith.

NERISSA

Then there is the County Palatine.

PORTIA

He doth nothing but frown, as who should say 'If you
will not have me, choose:' he hears merry tales and
smiles not: I fear he will prove the weeping
philosopher when he grows old, being so full of
unmannerly sadness in his youth. I had rather be
married to a death's-head with a bone in his mouth
than to either of these. God defend me from these
two!

NERISSA

How say you by the French lord, Monsieur Le Bon?

PORTIA

God made him, and therefore let him pass for a man.
In truth, I know it is a sin to be a mocker: but,
he! why, he hath a horse better than the
Neapolitan's, a better bad habit of frowning than
the Count Palatine; he is every man in no man; if a
throstle sing, he falls straight a capering: he will
fence with his own shadow: if I should marry him, I
should marry twenty husbands. If he would despise me
I would forgive him, for if he love me to madness, I
shall never requite him.

NERISSA

What say you, then, to Falconbridge, the young baron
of England?

PORTIA

You know I say nothing to him, for he understands
not me, nor I him: he hath neither Latin, French,
nor Italian, and you will come into the court and
swear that I have a poor pennyworth in the English.
He is a proper man's picture, but, alas, who can
converse with a dumb-show? How oddly he is suited!
I think he bought his doublet in Italy, his round
hose in France, his bonnet in Germany and his
behavior every where.

NERISSA

What think you of the Scottish lord, his neighbour?

PORTIA

That he hath a neighbourly charity in him, for he
borrowed a box of the ear of the Englishman and
swore he would pay him again when he was able: I
think the Frenchman became his surety and sealed
under for another.

NERISSA

How like you the young German, the Duke of Saxony's
nephew?

PORTIA

Very vilely in the morning, when he is sober, and
most vilely in the afternoon, when he is drunk: when
he is best, he is a little worse than a man, and
when he is worst, he is little better than a beast:
and the worst fall that ever fell, I hope I shall
make shift to go without him.

NERISSA

If he should offer to choose, and choose the right
casket, you should refuse to perform your father's
will, if you should refuse to accept him.

PORTIA

Therefore, for fear of the worst, I pray thee, set a
deep glass of rhenish wine on the contrary casket,
for if the devil be within and that temptation
without, I know he will choose it. I will do any
thing, Nerissa, ere I'll be married to a sponge.

NERISSA

You need not fear, lady, the having any of these
lords: they have acquainted me with their
determinations; which is, indeed, to return to their
home and to trouble you with no more suit, unless
you may be won by some other sort than your father's
imposition depending on the caskets.

PORTIA

If I live to be as old as Sibylla, I will die as
chaste as Diana, unless I be obtained by the manner
of my father's will. I am glad this parcel of wooers
are so reasonable, for there is not one among them
but I dote on his very absence, and I pray God grant
them a fair departure.

NERISSA

>Do you not remember, lady, in your father's time, a
>Venetian, a scholar and a soldier, that came hither
>in company of the Marquis of Montferrat?

PORTIA

>Yes, yes, it was Bassanio; as I think, he was so called.

NERISSA

>True, madam: he, of all the men that ever my foolish
>eyes looked upon, was the best deserving a fair lady.

PORTIA

>I remember him well, and I remember him worthy of
>thy praise.

Enter a Serving-man

>How now! what news?

Servant

>The four strangers seek for you, madam, to take
>their leave: and there is a forerunner come from a
>fifth, the Prince of Morocco, who brings word the
>prince his master will be here to-night.

PORTIA

>If I could bid the fifth welcome with so good a
>heart as I can bid the other four farewell, I should
>be glad of his approach: if he have the condition
>of a saint and the complexion of a devil, I had
>rather he should shrive me than wive me. Come,
>Nerissa. Sirrah, go before.
>Whiles we shut the gates
>upon one wooer, another knocks at the door.

Exeunt

SCENE III.

Venice. A public place.

Enter BASSANIO and SHYLOCK

SHYLOCK
Three thousand ducats; well.
BASSANIO
Ay, sir, for three months.
SHYLOCK
For three months; well.
BASSANIO
For the which, as I told you, Antonio shall be bound.
SHYLOCK
Antonio shall become bound; well.
BASSANIO
May you stead me? will you pleasure me? shall I
know your answer?
SHYLOCK
Three thousand ducats for three months and Antonio
bound.
BASSANIO
Your answer to that.
SHYLOCK
Antonio is a good man.
BASSANIO
Have you heard any imputation to the contrary?
SHYLOCK
Oh, no, no, no, no: my meaning in saying he is a
good man is to have you understand me that he is
sufficient. Yet his means are in supposition: he
hath an argosy bound to Tripolis, another to the
Indies; I understand moreover, upon the Rialto, he
hath a third at Mexico, a fourth for England, and
other ventures he hath, squandered abroad. But ships

are but boards, sailors but men: there be land-rats
and water-rats, water-thieves and land-thieves, I
mean pirates, and then there is the peril of waters,
winds and rocks. The man is, notwithstanding,
sufficient. Three thousand ducats; I think I may
take his bond.

BASSANIO

Be assured you may.

SHYLOCK

I will be assured I may; and, that I may be assured,
I will bethink me. May I speak with Antonio?

BASSANIO

If it please you to dine with us.

SHYLOCK

Yes, to smell pork; to eat of the habitation which
your prophet the Nazarite conjured the devil into. I
will buy with you, sell with you, talk with you,
walk with you, and so following, but I will not eat
with you, drink with you, nor pray with you. What
news on the Rialto? Who is he comes here?

Enter ANTONIO

BASSANIO

This is Signior Antonio.

SHYLOCK

[Aside] How like a fawning publican he looks!
I hate him for he is a Christian,
But more for that in low simplicity
He lends out money gratis and brings down
The rate of usance here with us in Venice.
If I can catch him once upon the hip,
I will feed fat the ancient grudge I bear him.
He hates our sacred nation, and he rails,
Even there where merchants most do congregate,

On me, my bargains and my well-won thrift,
Which he calls interest. Cursed be my tribe,
If I forgive him!

BASSANIO

Shylock, do you hear?

SHYLOCK

I am debating of my present store,
And, by the near guess of my memory,
I cannot instantly raise up the gross
Of full three thousand ducats. What of that?
Tubal, a wealthy Hebrew of my tribe,
Will furnish me. But soft! how many months
Do you desire?

To ANTONIO

Rest you fair, good signior;
Your worship was the last man in our mouths.

ANTONIO

Shylock, although I neither lend nor borrow
By taking nor by giving of excess,
Yet, to supply the ripe wants of my friend,
I'll break a custom. Is he yet possess'd
How much ye would?

SHYLOCK

Ay, ay, three thousand ducats.

ANTONIO

And for three months.

SHYLOCK

I had forgot; three months; you told me so.
Well then, your bond; and let me see; but hear you;
Methought you said you neither lend nor borrow
Upon advantage.

ANTONIO

I do never use it.

SHYLOCK
    When Jacob grazed his uncle Laban's sheep--
    This Jacob from our holy Abram was,
    As his wise mother wrought in his behalf,
    The third possessor; ay, he was the third--
ANTONIO
    And what of him? did he take interest?
SHYLOCK
    No, not take interest, not, as you would say,
    Directly interest: mark what Jacob did.
    When Laban and himself were compromised
    That all the eanlings which were streak'd and pied
    Should fall as Jacob's hire, the ewes, being rank,
    In the end of autumn turned to the rams,
    And, when the work of generation was
    Between these woolly breeders in the act,
    The skilful shepherd peel'd me certain wands,
    And, in the doing of the deed of kind,
    He stuck them up before the fulsome ewes,
    Who then conceiving did in eaning time
    Fall parti-colour'd lambs, and those were Jacob's.
    This was a way to thrive, and he was blest:
    And thrift is blessing, if men steal it not.
ANTONIO
    This was a venture, sir, that Jacob served for;
    A thing not in his power to bring to pass,
    But sway'd and fashion'd by the hand of heaven.
    Was this inserted to make interest good?
    Or is your gold and silver ewes and rams?
SHYLOCK
    I cannot tell; I make it breed as fast:
    But note me, signior.
ANTONIO
    Mark you this, Bassanio,

The devil can cite Scripture for his purpose.
An evil soul producing holy witness
Is like a villain with a smiling cheek,
A goodly apple rotten at the heart:
O, what a goodly outside falsehood hath!
SHYLOCK
Three thousand ducats; 'tis a good round sum.
Three months from twelve; then, let me see; the rate--
ANTONIO
Well, Shylock, shall we be beholding to you?
SHYLOCK
Signior Antonio, many a time and oft
In the Rialto you have rated me
About my moneys and my usances:
Still have I borne it with a patient shrug,
For sufferance is the badge of all our tribe.
You call me misbeliever, cut-throat dog,
And spit upon my Jewish gaberdine,
And all for use of that which is mine own.
Well then, it now appears you need my help:
Go to, then; you come to me, and you say
'Shylock, we would have moneys:' you say so;
You, that did void your rheum upon my beard
And foot me as you spurn a stranger cur
Over your threshold: moneys is your suit
What should I say to you? Should I not say
'Hath a dog money? is it possible
A cur can lend three thousand ducats?' Or
Shall I bend low and in a bondman's key,
With bated breath and whispering humbleness, Say this;
'Fair sir, you spit on me on Wednesday last;
You spurn'd me such a day; another time
You call'd me dog; and for these courtesies
I'll lend you thus much moneys'?

ANTONIO

    I am as like to call thee so again,
    To spit on thee again, to spurn thee too.
    If thou wilt lend this money, lend it not
    As to thy friends; for when did friendship take
    A breed for barren metal of his friend?
    But lend it rather to thine enemy,
    Who, if he break, thou mayst with better face
    Exact the penalty.

SHYLOCK

    Why, look you, how you storm!
    I would be friends with you and have your love,
    Forget the shames that you have stain'd me with,
    Supply your present wants and take no doit
    Of usance for my moneys, and you'll not hear me:
    This is kind I offer.

BASSANIO

    This were kindness.

SHYLOCK

    This kindness will I show.
    Go with me to a notary, seal me there
    Your single bond; and, in a merry sport,
    If you repay me not on such a day,
    In such a place, such sum or sums as are
    Express'd in the condition, let the forfeit
    Be nominated for an equal pound
    Of your fair flesh, to be cut off and taken
    In what part of your body pleaseth me.

ANTONIO

    Content, i' faith: I'll seal to such a bond
    And say there is much kindness in the Jew.

BASSANIO

    You shall not seal to such a bond for me:
    I'll rather dwell in my necessity.

ANTONIO

Why, fear not, man; I will not forfeit it:
Within these two months, that's a month before
This bond expires, I do expect return
Of thrice three times the value of this bond.

SHYLOCK

O father Abram, what these Christians are,
Whose own hard dealings teaches them suspect
The thoughts of others! Pray you, tell me this;
If he should break his day, what should I gain
By the exaction of the forfeiture?
A pound of man's flesh taken from a man
Is not so estimable, profitable neither,
As flesh of muttons, beefs, or goats. I say,
To buy his favour, I extend this friendship:
If he will take it, so; if not, adieu;
And, for my love, I pray you wrong me not.

ANTONIO

Yes Shylock, I will seal unto this bond.

SHYLOCK

Then meet me forthwith at the notary's;
Give him direction for this merry bond,
And I will go and purse the ducats straight,
See to my house, left in the fearful guard
Of an unthrifty knave, and presently
I will be with you.

ANTONIO

Hie thee, gentle Jew.

Exit Shylock

The Hebrew will turn Christian: he grows kind.

BASSANIO

I like not fair terms and a villain's mind.

ANTONIO
    Come on: in this there can be no dismay;
    My ships come home a month before the day.

Exeunt

ACT II

SCENE I.

Belmont. A room in PORTIA'S house.

Flourish of cornets. Enter the PRINCE OF MOROCCO and his train; PORTIA, NERISSA, and others attending

MOROCCO

Mislike me not for my complexion,
The shadow'd livery of the burnish'd sun,
To whom I am a neighbour and near bred.
Bring me the fairest creature northward born,
Where Phoebus' fire scarce thaws the icicles,
And let us make incision for your love,
To prove whose blood is reddest, his or mine.
I tell thee, lady, this aspect of mine
Hath fear'd the valiant: by my love I swear
The best-regarded virgins of our clime
Have loved it too: I would not change this hue,
Except to steal your thoughts, my gentle queen.

PORTIA

In terms of choice I am not solely led
By nice direction of a maiden's eyes;
Besides, the lottery of my destiny
Bars me the right of voluntary choosing:
But if my father had not scanted me
And hedged me by his wit, to yield myself
His wife who wins me by that means I told you,
Yourself, renowned prince, then stood as fair
As any comer I have look'd on yet
For my affection.

MOROCCO

Even for that I thank you:

Therefore, I pray you, lead me to the caskets
To try my fortune. By this scimitar
That slew the Sophy and a Persian prince
That won three fields of Sultan Solyman,
I would outstare the sternest eyes that look,
Outbrave the heart most daring on the earth,
Pluck the young sucking cubs from the she-bear,
Yea, mock the lion when he roars for prey,
To win thee, lady. But, alas the while!
If Hercules and Lichas play at dice
Which is the better man, the greater throw
May turn by fortune from the weaker hand:
So is Alcides beaten by his page;
And so may I, blind fortune leading me,
Miss that which one unworthier may attain,
And die with grieving.

PORTIA

You must take your chance,
And either not attempt to choose at all
Or swear before you choose, if you choose wrong
Never to speak to lady afterward
In way of marriage: therefore be advised.

MOROCCO

Nor will not. Come, bring me unto my chance.

PORTIA

First, forward to the temple: after dinner
Your hazard shall be made.

MOROCCO

Good fortune then!
To make me blest or cursed'st among men.

Cornets, and exeunt

SCENE II.

Venice. A street.

Enter LAUNCELOT

LAUNCELOT

Certainly my conscience will serve me to run from
this Jew my master. The fiend is at mine elbow and
tempts me saying to me 'Gobbo, Launcelot Gobbo, good
Launcelot,' or 'good Gobbo,' or good Launcelot
Gobbo, use your legs, take the start, run away. My
conscience says 'No; take heed,' honest Launcelot;
take heed, honest Gobbo, or, as aforesaid, 'honest
Launcelot Gobbo; do not run; scorn running with thy
heels.' Well, the most courageous fiend bids me
pack: 'Via!' says the fiend; 'away!' says the
fiend; 'for the heavens, rouse up a brave mind,'
says the fiend, 'and run.' Well, my conscience,
hanging about the neck of my heart, says very wisely
to me 'My honest friend Launcelot, being an honest
man's son,' or rather an honest woman's son; for,
indeed, my father did something smack, something
grow to, he had a kind of taste; well, my conscience
says 'Launcelot, budge not.' 'Budge,' says the
fiend. 'Budge not,' says my conscience.
'Conscience,' say I, 'you counsel well;' ' Fiend,'
say I, 'you counsel well:' to be ruled by my
conscience, I should stay with the Jew my master,
who, God bless the mark, is a kind of devil; and, to
run away from the Jew, I should be ruled by the
fiend, who, saving your reverence, is the devil
himself. Certainly the Jew is the very devil
incarnal; and, in my conscience, my conscience is
but a kind of hard conscience, to offer to counsel
me to stay with the Jew. The fiend gives the more

friendly counsel: I will run, fiend; my heels are
at your command; I will run.

Enter Old GOBBO, with a basket

GOBBO

Master young man, you, I pray you, which is the way
to master Jew's?

LAUNCELOT

[Aside] O heavens, this is my true-begotten father!
who, being more than sand-blind, high-gravel blind,
knows me not: I will try confusions with him.

GOBBO

Master young gentleman, I pray you, which is the way
to master Jew's?

LAUNCELOT

Turn up on your right hand at the next turning, but,
at the next turning of all, on your left; marry, at
the very next turning, turn of no hand, but turn
down indirectly to the Jew's house.

GOBBO

By God's sonties, 'twill be a hard way to hit. Can
you tell me whether one Launcelot,
that dwells with him, dwell with him or no?

LAUNCELOT

Talk you of young Master Launcelot?

Aside

Mark me now; now will I raise the waters. Talk you
of young Master Launcelot?

GOBBO

No master, sir, but a poor man's son: his father,
though I say it, is an honest exceeding poor man
and, God be thanked, well to live.

LAUNCELOT

Well, let his father be what a' will, we talk of
young Master Launcelot.

GOBBO

Your worship's friend and Launcelot, sir.

LAUNCELOT

But I pray you, ergo, old man, ergo, I beseech you,
talk you of young Master Launcelot?

GOBBO

Of Launcelot, an't please your mastership.

LAUNCELOT

Ergo, Master Launcelot. Talk not of Master
Launcelot, father; for the young gentleman,
according to Fates and Destinies and such odd
sayings, the Sisters Three and such branches of
learning, is indeed deceased, or, as you would say
in plain terms, gone to heaven.

GOBBO

Marry, God forbid! the boy was the very staff of my
age, my very prop.

LAUNCELOT

Do I look like a cudgel or a hovel-post, a staff or
a prop? Do you know me, father?

GOBBO

Alack the day, I know you not, young gentleman:
but, I pray you, tell me, is my boy, God rest his
soul, alive or dead?

LAUNCELOT

Do you not know me, father?

GOBBO

Alack, sir, I am sand-blind; I know you not.

LAUNCELOT

Nay, indeed, if you had your eyes, you might fail of
the knowing me: it is a wise father that knows his

own child. Well, old man, I will tell you news of
your son: give me your blessing: truth will come
to light; murder cannot be hid long; a man's son
may, but at the length truth will out.

GOBBO

Pray you, sir, stand up: I am sure you are not
Launcelot, my boy.

LAUNCELOT

Pray you, let's have no more fooling about it, but
give me your blessing: I am Launcelot, your boy
that was, your son that is, your child that shall
be.

GOBBO

I cannot think you are my son.

LAUNCELOT

I know not what I shall think of that: but I am
Launcelot, the Jew's man, and I am sure Margery your
wife is my mother.

GOBBO

Her name is Margery, indeed: I'll be sworn, if thou
be Launcelot, thou art mine own flesh and blood.
Lord worshipped might he be! what a beard hast thou
got! thou hast got more hair on thy chin than
Dobbin my fill-horse has on his tail.

LAUNCELOT

It should seem, then, that Dobbin's tail grows
backward: I am sure he had more hair of his tail
than I have of my face when I last saw him.

GOBBO

Lord, how art thou changed! How dost thou and thy
master agree? I have brought him a present. How
'gree you now?

LAUNCELOT

Well, well: but, for mine own part, as I have set

up my rest to run away, so I will not rest till I
have run some ground. My master's a very Jew: give
him a present! give him a halter: I am famished in
his service; you may tell every finger I have with
my ribs. Father, I am glad you are come: give me
your present to one Master Bassanio, who, indeed,
gives rare new liveries: if I serve not him, I
will run as far as God has any ground. O rare
fortune! here comes the man: to him, father; for I
am a Jew, if I serve the Jew any longer.

Enter BASSANIO, with LEONARDO and other followers

BASSANIO
You may do so; but let it be so hasted that supper
be ready at the farthest by five of the clock. See
these letters delivered; put the liveries to making,
and desire Gratiano to come anon to my lodging.

Exit a Servant

LAUNCELOT
To him, father.
GOBBO
God bless your worship!
BASSANIO
Gramercy! wouldst thou aught with me?
GOBBO
Here's my son, sir, a poor boy,--
LAUNCELOT
Not a poor boy, sir, but the rich Jew's man; that
would, sir, as my father shall specify--
GOBBO
He hath a great infection, sir, as one would say, to
serve--

LAUNCELOT

Indeed, the short and the long is, I serve the Jew,
and have a desire, as my father shall specify--

GOBBO

His master and he, saving your worship's reverence,
are scarce cater-cousins--

LAUNCELOT

To be brief, the very truth is that the Jew, having
done me wrong, doth cause me, as my father, being, I
hope, an old man, shall frutify unto you--

GOBBO

I have here a dish of doves that I would bestow upon
your worship, and my suit is--

LAUNCELOT

In very brief, the suit is impertinent to myself, as
your worship shall know by this honest old man; and,
though I say it, though old man, yet poor man, my
father.

BASSANIO

One speak for both. What would you?

LAUNCELOT

Serve you, sir.

GOBBO

That is the very defect of the matter, sir.

BASSANIO

I know thee well; thou hast obtain'd thy suit:
Shylock thy master spoke with me this day,
And hath preferr'd thee, if it be preferment
To leave a rich Jew's service, to become
The follower of so poor a gentleman.

LAUNCELOT

The old proverb is very well parted between my
master Shylock and you, sir: you have the grace of
God, sir, and he hath enough.

BASSANIO

Thou speak'st it well. Go, father, with thy son.
Take leave of thy old master and inquire
My lodging out. Give him a livery
More guarded than his fellows': see it done.

LAUNCELOT

Father, in. I cannot get a service, no; I have
ne'er a tongue in my head. Well, if any man in
Italy have a fairer table which doth offer to swear
upon a book, I shall have good fortune. Go to,
here's a simple line of life: here's a small trifle
of wives: alas, fifteen wives is nothing! eleven
widows and nine maids is a simple coming-in for one
man: and then to 'scape drowning thrice, and to be
in peril of my life with the edge of a feather-bed;
here are simple scapes. Well, if Fortune be a
woman, she's a good wench for this gear. Father,
come; I'll take my leave of the Jew in the twinkling of
an eye.

Exeunt Launcelot and Old Gobbo

BASSANIO

I pray thee, good Leonardo, think on this:
These things being bought and orderly bestow'd,
Return in haste, for I do feast to-night
My best-esteem'd acquaintance: hie thee, go.

LEONARDO

My best endeavours shall be done herein.

Enter GRATIANO

GRATIANO

Where is your master?

LEONARDO

Yonder, sir, he walks.

Exit

GRATIANO
Signior Bassanio!
BASSANIO
Gratiano!
GRATIANO
I have a suit to you.
BASSANIO
You have obtain'd it.
GRATIANO
You must not deny me: I must go with you to Belmont.
BASSANIO
Why then you must. But hear thee, Gratiano;
Thou art too wild, too rude and bold of voice;
Parts that become thee happily enough
And in such eyes as ours appear not faults;
But where thou art not known, why, there they show
Something too liberal. Pray thee, take pain
To allay with some cold drops of modesty
Thy skipping spirit, lest through thy wild behavior
I be misconstrued in the place I go to,
And lose my hopes.
GRATIANO
Signior Bassanio, hear me:
If I do not put on a sober habit,
Talk with respect and swear but now and then,
Wear prayer-books in my pocket, look demurely,
Nay more, while grace is saying, hood mine eyes
Thus with my hat, and sigh and say 'amen,'
Use all the observance of civility,
Like one well studied in a sad ostent
To please his grandam, never trust me more.

35

BASSANIO

    Well, we shall see your bearing.

GRATIANO

    Nay, but I bar to-night: you shall not gauge me

    By what we do to-night.

BASSANIO

    No, that were pity:

    I would entreat you rather to put on

    Your boldest suit of mirth, for we have friends

    That purpose merriment. But fare you well:

    I have some business.

GRATIANO

    And I must to Lorenzo and the rest:

    But we will visit you at supper-time.

Exeunt

SCENE III.

The same. A room in SHYLOCK'S house.

Enter JESSICA and LAUNCELOT

JESSICA

    I am sorry thou wilt leave my father so:

    Our house is hell, and thou, a merry devil,

    Didst rob it of some taste of tediousness.

    But fare thee well, there is a ducat for thee:

    And, Launcelot, soon at supper shalt thou see

    Lorenzo, who is thy new master's guest:

    Give him this letter; do it secretly;

    And so farewell: I would not have my father

    See me in talk with thee.

LAUNCELOT

    Adieu! tears exhibit my tongue. Most beautiful

    pagan, most sweet Jew! if a Christian did not play

the knave and get thee, I am much deceived. But,
adieu: these foolish drops do something drown my
manly spirit: adieu.
JESSICA
Farewell, good Launcelot.

Exit Launcelot

Alack, what heinous sin is it in me
To be ashamed to be my father's child!
But though I am a daughter to his blood,
I am not to his manners. O Lorenzo,
If thou keep promise, I shall end this strife,
Become a Christian and thy loving wife.

Exit

SCENE IV.

The same. A street.

Enter GRATIANO, LORENZO, SALARINO, and SALANIO

LORENZO
Nay, we will slink away in supper-time,
Disguise us at my lodging and return,
All in an hour.
GRATIANO
We have not made good preparation.
SALARINO
We have not spoke us yet of torchbearers.
SALANIO
'Tis vile, unless it may be quaintly order'd,
And better in my mind not undertook.
LORENZO
'Tis now but four o'clock: we have two hours

To furnish us.

Enter LAUNCELOT, with a letter

Friend Launcelot, what's the news?
LAUNCELOT
    An it shall please you to break up
    this, it shall seem to signify.
LORENZO
    I know the hand: in faith, 'tis a fair hand;
    And whiter than the paper it writ on
    Is the fair hand that writ.
GRATIANO
    Love-news, in faith.
LAUNCELOT
    By your leave, sir.
LORENZO
    Whither goest thou?
LAUNCELOT
    Marry, sir, to bid my old master the
    Jew to sup to-night with my new master the Christian.
LORENZO
    Hold here, take this: tell gentle Jessica
    I will not fail her; speak it privately.
    Go, gentlemen,

Exit Launcelot

Will you prepare you for this masque tonight?
I am provided of a torch-bearer.
SALANIO
    Ay, marry, I'll be gone about it straight.
SALANIO
    And so will I.
LORENZO

Meet me and Gratiano
At Gratiano's lodging some hour hence.
SALARINO
'Tis good we do so.

Exeunt SALARINO and SALANIO

GRATIANO
Was not that letter from fair Jessica?
LORENZO
I must needs tell thee all. She hath directed
How I shall take her from her father's house,
What gold and jewels she is furnish'd with,
What page's suit she hath in readiness.
If e'er the Jew her father come to heaven,
It will be for his gentle daughter's sake:
And never dare misfortune cross her foot,
Unless she do it under this excuse,
That she is issue to a faithless Jew.
Come, go with me; peruse this as thou goest:
Fair Jessica shall be my torch-beare r.

Exeunt

SCENE V.

The same. Before SHYLOCK'S house.

Enter SHYLOCK and LAUNCELOT

SHYLOCK
Well, thou shalt see, thy eyes shall be thy judge,
The difference of old Shylock and Bassanio:--
What, Jessica!--thou shalt not gormandise,
As thou hast done with me:--What, Jessica!--
And sleep and snore, and rend apparel out;--

Why, Jessica, I say!
LAUNCELOT
Why, Jessica!
SHYLOCK
Who bids thee call? I do not bid thee call.
LAUNCELOT
Your worship was wont to tell me that
I could do nothing without bidding.

Enter Jessica

JESSICA
Call you? what is your will?
SHYLOCK
I am bid forth to supper, Jessica:
There are my keys. But wherefore should I go?
I am not bid for love; they flatter me:
But yet I'll go in hate, to feed upon
The prodigal Christian. Jessica, my girl,
Look to my house. I am right loath to go:
There is some ill a-brewing towards my rest,
For I did dream of money-bags to-night.
LAUNCELOT
I beseech you, sir, go: my young master doth expect
your reproach.
SHYLOCK
So do I his.
LAUNCELOT
An they have conspired together, I will not say you
shall see a masque; but if you do, then it was not
for nothing that my nose fell a-bleeding on
Black-Monday last at six o'clock i' the morning,
falling out that year on Ash-Wednesday was four
year, in the afternoon.
SHYLOCK

What, are there masques? Hear you me, Jessica:
Lock up my doors; and when you hear the drum
And the vile squealing of the wry-neck'd fife,
Clamber not you up to the casements then,
Nor thrust your head into the public street
To gaze on Christian fools with varnish'd faces,
But stop my house's ears, I mean my casements:
Let not the sound of shallow foppery enter
My sober house. By Jacob's staff, I swear,
I have no mind of feasting forth to-night:
But I will go. Go you before me, sirrah;
Say I will come.

LAUNCELOT

I will go before, sir. Mistress, look out at
window, for all this, There will come a Christian
boy, will be worth a Jewess' eye.

Exit

SHYLOCK

What says that fool of Hagar's offspring, ha?

JESSICA

His words were 'Farewell mistress;' nothing else.

SHYLOCK

The patch is kind enough, but a huge feeder;
Snail-slow in profit, and he sleeps by day
More than the wild-cat: drones hive not with me;
Therefore I part with him, and part with him
To one that would have him help to waste
His borrow'd purse. Well, Jessica, go in;
Perhaps I will return immediately:
Do as I bid you; shut doors after you:
Fast bind, fast find;
A proverb never stale in thrifty mind.

41

Exit

JESSICA

Farewell; and if my fortune be not crost,
I have a father, you a daughter, lost.

Exit

SCENE VI.

The same.

Enter GRATIANO and SALARINO, masqued

GRATIANO

This is the pent-house under which Lorenzo
Desired us to make stand.

SALARINO

His hour is almost past.

GRATIANO

And it is marvel he out-dwells his hour,
For lovers ever run before the clock.

SALARINO

O, ten times faster Venus' pigeons fly
To seal love's bonds new-made, than they are wont
To keep obliged faith unforfeited!

GRATIANO

That ever holds: who riseth from a feast
With that keen appetite that he sits down?
Where is the horse that doth untread again
His tedious measures with the unbated fire
That he did pace them first? All things that are,
Are with more spirit chased than enjoy'd.
How like a younker or a prodigal
The scarfed bark puts from her native bay,
Hugg'd and embraced by the strumpet wind!

How like the prodigal doth she return,
With over-weather'd ribs and ragged sails,
Lean, rent and beggar'd by the strumpet wind!
SALARINO
Here comes Lorenzo: more of this hereafter.

Enter LORENZO

LORENZO
Sweet friends, your patience for my long abode;
Not I, but my affairs, have made you wait:
When you shall please to play the thieves for wives,
I'll watch as long for you then. Approach;
Here dwells my father Jew. Ho! who's within?

Enter JESSICA, above, in boy's clothes

JESSICA
Who are you? Tell me, for more certainty,
Albeit I'll swear that I do know your tongue.
LORENZO
Lorenzo, and thy love.
JESSICA
Lorenzo, certain, and my love indeed,
For who love I so much? And now who knows
But you, Lorenzo, whether I am yours?
LORENZO
Heaven and thy thoughts are witness that thou art.
JESSICA
Here, catch this casket; it is worth the pains.
I am glad 'tis night, you do not look on me,
For I am much ashamed of my exchange:
But love is blind and lovers cannot see
The pretty follies that themselves commit;
For if they could, Cupid himself would blush

To see me thus transformed to a boy.
LORENZO
Descend, for you must be my torchbearer.
JESSICA
What, must I hold a candle to my shames?
They in themselves, good-sooth, are too too light.
Why, 'tis an office of discovery, love;
And I should be obscured.
LORENZO
So are you, sweet,
Even in the lovely garnish of a boy.
But come at once;
For the close night doth play the runaway,
And we are stay'd for at Bassanio's feast.
JESSICA
I will make fast the doors, and gild myself
With some more ducats, and be with you straight.

Exit above

GRATIANO
Now, by my hood, a Gentile and no Jew.
LORENZO
Beshrew me but I love her heartily;
For she is wise, if I can judge of her,
And fair she is, if that mine eyes be true,
And true she is, as she hath proved herself,
And therefore, like herself, wise, fair and true,
Shall she be placed in my constant soul.

Enter JESSICA, below

What, art thou come? On, gentlemen; away!
Our masquing mates by this time for us stay.

Exit with Jessica and Salarino

Enter ANTONIO

ANTONIO
    Who's there?
GRATIANO
    Signior Antonio!
ANTONIO
    Fie, fie, Gratiano! where are all the rest?
    'Tis nine o'clock: our friends all stay for you.
    No masque to-night: the wind is come about;
    Bassanio presently will go aboard:
    I have sent twenty out to seek for you.
GRATIANO
    I am glad on't: I desire no more delight
    Than to be under sail and gone to-night.

Exeunt

SCENE VII.

Belmont. A room in PORTIA'S house.

*Flourish of cornets. Enter PORTIA, with the PRINCE OF
MOROCCO, and their trains*

PORTIA
    Go draw aside the curtains and discover
    The several caskets to this noble prince.
    Now make your choice.
MOROCCO
    The first, of gold, who this inscription bears,
    'Who chooseth me shall gain what many men desire;'
    The second, silver, which this promise carries,
    'Who chooseth me shall get as much as he deserves;'
    This third, dull lead, with warning all as blunt,

'Who chooseth me must give and hazard all he hath.'
How shall I know if I do choose the right?
PORTIA
The one of them contains my picture, prince:
If you choose that, then I am yours withal.
MOROCCO
Some god direct my judgment! Let me see;
I will survey the inscriptions back again.
What says this leaden casket?
'Who chooseth me must give and hazard all he hath.'
Must give: for what? for lead? hazard for lead?
This casket threatens. Men that hazard all
Do it in hope of fair advantages:
A golden mind stoops not to shows of dross;
I'll then nor give nor hazard aught for lead.
What says the silver with her virgin hue?
'Who chooseth me shall get as much as he deserves.'
As much as he deserves! Pause there, Morocco,
And weigh thy value with an even hand:
If thou be'st rated by thy estimation,
Thou dost deserve enough; and yet enough
May not extend so far as to the lady:
And yet to be afeard of my deserving
Were but a weak disabling of myself.
As much as I deserve! Why, that's the lady:
I do in birth deserve her, and in fortunes,
In graces and in qualities of breeding;
But more than these, in love I do deserve.
What if I stray'd no further, but chose here?
Let's see once more this saying graved in gold
'Who chooseth me shall gain what many men desire.'
Why, that's the lady; all the world desires her;
From the four corners of the earth they come,
To kiss this shrine, this mortal-breathing saint:

The Hyrcanian deserts and the vasty wilds
Of wide Arabia are as thoroughfares now
For princes to come view fair Portia:
The watery kingdom, whose ambitious head
Spits in the face of heaven, is no bar
To stop the foreign spirits, but they come,
As o'er a brook, to see fair Portia.
One of these three contains her heavenly picture.
Is't like that lead contains her? 'Twere damnation
To think so base a thought: it were too gross
To rib her cerecloth in the obscure grave.
Or shall I think in silver she's immured,
Being ten times undervalued to tried gold?
O sinful thought! Never so rich a gem
Was set in worse than gold. They have in England
A coin that bears the figure of an angel
Stamped in gold, but that's insculp'd upon;
But here an angel in a golden bed
Lies all within. Deliver me the key:
Here do I choose, and thrive I as I may!
PORTIA
There, take it, prince; and if my form lie there,
Then I am yours.

He unlocks the golden casket

MOROCCO
O hell! what have we here?
A carrion Death, within whose empty eye
There is a written scroll! I'll read the writing.

Reads

All that glitters is not gold;
Often have you heard that told:

Many a man his life hath sold
But my outside to behold:
Gilded tombs do worms enfold.
Had you been as wise as bold,
Young in limbs, in judgment old,
Your answer had not been inscroll'd:
Fare you well; your suit is cold.
Cold, indeed; and labour lost:
Then, farewell, heat, and welcome, frost!
Portia, adieu. I have too grieved a heart
To take a tedious leave: thus losers part.

Exit with his train. Flourish of cornets

PORTIA
A gentle riddance. Draw the curtains, go.
Let all of his complexion choose me so.

Exeunt

SCENE VIII.

Venice. A street.

Enter SALARINO and SALANIO

SALARINO
Why, man, I saw Bassanio under sail:
With him is Gratiano gone along;
And in their ship I am sure Lorenzo is not.
SALANIO
The villain Jew with outcries raised the duke,
Who went with him to search Bassanio's ship.
SALARINO
He came too late, the ship was under sail:

But there the duke was given to understand
That in a gondola were seen together
Lorenzo and his amorous Jessica:
Besides, Antonio certified the duke
They were not with Bassanio in his ship.

SALANIO
I never heard a passion so confused,
So strange, outrageous, and so variable,
As the dog Jew did utter in the streets:
'My daughter! O my ducats! O my daughter!
Fled with a Christian! O my Christian ducats!
Justice! the law! my ducats, and my daughter!
A sealed bag, two sealed bags of ducats,
Of double ducats, stolen from me by my daughter!
And jewels, two stones, two rich and precious stones,
Stolen by my daughter! Justice! find the girl;
She hath the stones upon her, and the ducats.'

SALARINO
Why, all the boys in Venice follow him,
Crying, his stones, his daughter, and his ducats.

SALANIO
Let good Antonio look he keep his day,
Or he shall pay for this.

SALARINO
Marry, well remember'd.
I reason'd with a Frenchman yesterday,
Who told me, in the narrow seas that part
The French and English, there miscarried
A vessel of our country richly fraught:
I thought upon Antonio when he told me;
And wish'd in silence that it were not his.

SALANIO
You were best to tell Antonio what you hear;
Yet do not suddenly, for it may grieve him.

SALARINO

    A kinder gentleman treads not the earth.
    I saw Bassanio and Antonio part:
    Bassanio told him he would make some speed
    Of his return: he answer'd, 'Do not so;
    Slubber not business for my sake, Bassanio
    But stay the very riping of the time;
    And for the Jew's bond which he hath of me,
    Let it not enter in your mind of love:
    Be merry, and employ your chiefest thoughts
    To courtship and such fair ostents of love
    As shall conveniently become you there:'
    And even there, his eye being big with tears,
    Turning his face, he put his hand behind him,
    And with affection wondrous sensible
    He wrung Bassanio's hand; and so they parted.

SALANIO

    I think he only loves the world for him.
    I pray thee, let us go and find him out
    And quicken his embraced heaviness
    With some delight or other.

SALARINO

    Do we so.

Exeunt

SCENE IX.

Belmont. A room in PORTIA'S house.

Enter NERISSA with a Servitor

NERISSA

    Quick, quick, I pray thee; draw the curtain straight:
    The Prince of Arragon hath ta'en his oath,
    And comes to his election presently.

Flourish of cornets. Enter the PRINCE OF ARRAGON,
PORTIA, and their trains

PORTIA

    Behold, there stand the caskets, noble prince:
    If you choose that wherein I am contain'd,
    Straight shall our nuptial rites be solemnized:
    But if you fail, without more speech, my lord,
    You must be gone from hence immediately.

ARRAGON

    I am enjoin'd by oath to observe three things:
    First, never to unfold to any one
    Which casket 'twas I chose; next, if I fail
    Of the right casket, never in my life
    To woo a maid in way of marriage: Lastly,
    If I do fail in fortune of my choice,
    Immediately to leave you and be gone.

PORTIA

    To these injunctions every one doth swear
    That comes to hazard for my worthless self.

ARRAGON

    And so have I address'd me. Fortune now
    To my heart's hope! Gold; silver; and base lead.
    'Who chooseth me must give and hazard all he hath.'
    You shall look fairer, ere I give or hazard.
    What says the golden chest? ha! let me see:
    'Who chooseth me shall gain what many men desire.'
    What many men desire! that 'many' may be meant
    By the fool multitude, that choose by show,
    Not learning more than the fond eye doth teach;
    Which pries not to the interior, but, like the martlet,
    Builds in the weather on the outward wall,
    Even in the force and road of casualty.
    I will not choose what many men desire,

Because I will not jump with common spirits
And rank me with the barbarous multitudes.
Why, then to thee, thou silver treasure-house;
Tell me once more what title thou dost bear:
'Who chooseth me shall get as much as he deserves:'
And well said too; for who shall go about
To cozen fortune and be honourable
Without the stamp of merit? Let none presume
To wear an undeserved dignity.
O, that estates, degrees and offices
Were not derived corruptly, and that clear honour
Were purchased by the merit of the wearer!
How many then should cover that stand bare!
How many be commanded that command!
How much low peasantry would then be glean'd
From the true seed of honour! and how much honour
Pick'd from the chaff and ruin of the times
To be new-varnish'd! Well, but to my choice:
'Who chooseth me shall get as much as he deserves.'
I will assume desert. Give me a key for this,
And instantly unlock my fortunes here.

He opens the silver casket

PORTIA
  Too long a pause for that which you find there.
ARRAGON
  What's here? the portrait of a blinking idiot,
  Presenting me a schedule! I will read it.
  How much unlike art thou to Portia!
  How much unlike my hopes and my deservings!
  'Who chooseth me shall have as much as he deserves.'
  Did I deserve no more than a fool's head?
  Is that my prize? are my deserts no better?
PORTIA

To offend, and judge, are distinct offices
And of opposed natures.
ARRAGON
What is here?

Reads

The fire seven times tried this:
Seven times tried that judgment is,
That did never choose amiss.
Some there be that shadows kiss;
Such have but a shadow's bliss:
There be fools alive, I wis,
Silver'd o'er; and so was this.
Take what wife you will to bed,
I will ever be your head:
So be gone: you are sped.
Still more fool I shall appear
By the time I linger here
With one fool's head I came to woo,
But I go away with two.
Sweet, adieu. I'll keep my oath,
Patiently to bear my wroth.

Exeunt Arragon and train

PORTIA
Thus hath the candle singed the moth.
O, these deliberate fools! when they do choose,
They have the wisdom by their wit to lose.
NERISSA
The ancient saying is no heresy,
Hanging and wiving goes by destiny.
PORTIA
Come, draw the curtain, Nerissa.

Enter a Servant

Servant
  Where is my lady?
PORTIA
  Here: what would my lord?
Servant
  Madam, there is alighted at your gate
  A young Venetian, one that comes before
  To signify the approaching of his lord;
  From whom he bringeth sensible regreets,
  To wit, besides commends and courteous breath,
  Gifts of rich value. Yet I have not seen
  So likely an ambassador of love:
  A day in April never came so sweet,
  To show how costly summer was at hand,
  As this fore-spurrer comes before his lord.
PORTIA
  No more, I pray thee: I am half afeard
  Thou wilt say anon he is some kin to thee,
  Thou spend'st such high-day wit in praising him.
  Come, come, Nerissa; for I long to see
  Quick Cupid's post that comes so mannerly.
NERISSA
  Bassanio, lord Love, if thy will it be!

Exeunt

ACT III

SCENE I.

Venice. A street.

Enter SALANIO and SALARINO

SALANIO

Now, what news on the Rialto?

SALARINO

Why, yet it lives there uncheck'd that Antonio hath
a ship of rich lading wrecked on the narrow seas;
the Goodwins, I think they call the place; a very
dangerous flat and fatal, where the carcasses of many
a tall ship lie buried, as they say, if my gossip
Report be an honest woman of her word.

SALANIO

I would she were as lying a gossip in that as ever
knapped ginger or made her neighbours believe she
wept for the death of a third husband. But it is
true, without any slips of prolixity or crossing the
plain highway of talk, that the good Antonio, the
honest Antonio,--O that I had a title good enough
to keep his name company!--

SALARINO

Come, the full stop.

SALANIO

Ha! what sayest thou? Why, the end is, he hath
lost a ship.

SALARINO

I would it might prove the end of his losses.

SALANIO

Let me say 'amen' betimes, lest the devil cross my
prayer, for here he comes in the likeness of a Jew.

Enter SHYLOCK

How now, Shylock! what news among the merchants?
SHYLOCK

You know, none so well, none so well as you, of my
daughter's flight.
SALARINO

That's certain: I, for my part, knew the tailor
that made the wings she flew withal.
SALANIO

And Shylock, for his own part, knew the bird was
fledged; and then it is the complexion of them all
to leave the dam.
SHYLOCK

She is damned for it.
SALANIO

That's certain, if the devil may be her judge.
SHYLOCK

My own flesh and blood to rebel!
SALANIO

Out upon it, old carrion! rebels it at these years?
SHYLOCK

I say, my daughter is my flesh and blood.
SALARINO

There is more difference between thy flesh and hers
than between jet and ivory; more between your bloods
than there is between red wine and rhenish. But
tell us, do you hear whether Antonio have had any
loss at sea or no?
SHYLOCK

There I have another bad match: a bankrupt, a
prodigal, who dare scarce show his head on the
Rialto; a beggar, that was used to come so smug upon
the mart; let him look to his bond: he was wont to

call me usurer; let him look to his bond: he was
wont to lend money for a Christian courtesy; let him
look to his bond.

SALARINO

Why, I am sure, if he forfeit, thou wilt not take
his flesh: what's that good for?

SHYLOCK

To bait fish withal: if it will feed nothing else,
it will feed my revenge. He hath disgraced me, and
hindered me half a million; laughed at my losses,
mocked at my gains, scorned my nation, thwarted my
bargains, cooled my friends, heated mine
enemies; and what's his reason? I am a Jew. Hath
not a Jew eyes? hath not a Jew hands, organs,
dimensions, senses, affections, passions? fed with
the same food, hurt with the same weapons, subject
to the same diseases, healed by the same means,
warmed and cooled by the same winter and summer, as
a Christian is? If you prick us, do we not bleed?
if you tickle us, do we not laugh? if you poison
us, do we not die? and if you wrong us, shall we not
revenge? If we are like you in the rest, we will
resemble you in that. If a Jew wrong a Christian,
what is his humility? Revenge. If a Christian
wrong a Jew, what should his sufferance be by
Christian example? Why, revenge. The villany you
teach me, I will execute, and it shall go hard but I
will better the instruction.

Enter a Servant

Servant

Gentlemen, my master Antonio is at his house and
desires to speak with you both.

SALARINO

We have been up and down to seek him.

Enter TUBAL

SALANIO

Here comes another of the tribe: a third cannot be
matched, unless the devil himself turn Jew.

Exeunt SALANIO, SALARINO, and Servant

SHYLOCK

How now, Tubal! what news from Genoa? hast thou
found my daughter?

TUBAL

I often came where I did hear of her, but cannot find her.

SHYLOCK

Why, there, there, there, there! a diamond gone,
cost me two thousand ducats in Frankfort! The curse
never fell upon our nation till now; I never felt it
till now: two thousand ducats in that; and other
precious, precious jewels. I would my daughter
were dead at my foot, and the jewels in her ear!
would she were hearsed at my foot, and the ducats in
her coffin! No news of them? Why, so: and I know
not what's spent in the search: why, thou loss upon
loss! the thief gone with so much, and so much to
find the thief; and no satisfaction, no revenge:
nor no in luck stirring but what lights on my
shoulders; no sighs but of my breathing; no tears
but of my shedding.

TUBAL

Yes, other men have ill luck too: Antonio, as I
heard in Genoa,--

SHYLOCK

What, what, what? ill luck, ill luck?

TUBAL

Hath an argosy cast away, coming from Tripolis.

SHYLOCK

I thank God, I thank God. Is't true, is't true?

TUBAL

I spoke with some of the sailors that escaped the wreck.

SHYLOCK

I thank thee, good Tubal: good news, good news!
ha, ha! where? in Genoa?

TUBAL

Your daughter spent in Genoa, as I heard, in one
night fourscore ducats.

SHYLOCK

Thou stickest a dagger in me: I shall never see my
gold again: fourscore ducats at a sitting!
fourscore ducats!

TUBAL

There came divers of Antonio's creditors in my
company to Venice, that swear he cannot choose but
break.

SHYLOCK

I am very glad of it: I'll plague him; I'll torture
him: I am glad of it.

TUBAL

One of them showed me a ring that he had of your
daughter for a monkey.

SHYLOCK

Out upon her! Thou torturest me, Tubal: it was my
turquoise; I had it of Leah when I was a bachelor:
I would not have given it for a wilderness of monkeys.

TUBAL

But Antonio is certainly undone.

SHYLOCK

Nay, that's true, that's very true. Go, Tubal, fee

me an officer; bespeak him a fortnight before. I
will have the heart of him, if he forfeit; for, were
he out of Venice, I can make what merchandise I
will. Go, go, Tubal, and meet me at our synagogue;
go, good Tubal; at our synagogue, Tubal.

Exeunt

SCENE II.

Belmont. A room in PORTIA'S house.

Enter BASSANIO, PORTIA, GRATIANO, NERISSA, and
Attendants

PORTIA
    I pray you, tarry: pause a day or two
    Before you hazard; for, in choosing wrong,
    I lose your company: therefore forbear awhile.
    There's something tells me, but it is not love,
    I would not lose you; and you know yourself,
    Hate counsels not in such a quality.
    But lest you should not understand me well,--
    And yet a maiden hath no tongue but thought,--
    I would detain you here some month or two
    Before you venture for me. I could teach you
    How to choose right, but I am then forsworn;
    So will I never be: so may you miss me;
    But if you do, you'll make me wish a sin,
    That I had been forsworn. Beshrew your eyes,
    They have o'erlook'd me and divided me;
    One half of me is yours, the other half yours,
    Mine own, I would say; but if mine, then yours,
    And so all yours. O, these naughty times
    Put bars between the owners and their rights!
    And so, though yours, not yours. Prove it so,

Let fortune go to hell for it, not I.
I speak too long; but 'tis to peize the time,
To eke it and to draw it out in length,
To stay you from election.
BASSANIO
Let me choose
For as I am, I live upon the rack.
PORTIA
Upon the rack, Bassanio! then confess
What treason there is mingled with your love.
BASSANIO
None but that ugly treason of mistrust,
Which makes me fear the enjoying of my love:
There may as well be amity and life
'Tween snow and fire, as treason and my love.
PORTIA
Ay, but I fear you speak upon the rack,
Where men enforced do speak anything.
BASSANIO
Promise me life, and I'll confess the truth.
PORTIA
Well then, confess and live.
BASSANIO
'Confess' and 'love'
Had been the very sum of my confession:
O happy torment, when my torturer
Doth teach me answers for deliverance!
But let me to my fortune and the caskets.
PORTIA
Away, then! I am lock'd in one of them:
If you do love me, you will find me out.
Nerissa and the rest, stand all aloof.
Let music sound while he doth make his choice;
Then, if he lose, he makes a swan-like end,

Fading in music: that the comparison
May stand more proper, my eye shall be the stream
And watery death-bed for him. He may win;
And what is music then? Then music is
Even as the flourish when true subjects bow
To a new-crowned monarch: such it is
As are those dulcet sounds in break of day
That creep into the dreaming bridegroom's ear,
And summon him to marriage. Now he goes,
With no less presence, but with much more love,
Than young Alcides, when he did redeem
The virgin tribute paid by howling Troy
To the sea-monster: I stand for sacrifice
The rest aloof are the Dardanian wives,
With bleared visages, come forth to view
The issue of the exploit. Go, Hercules!
Live thou, I live: with much, much more dismay
I view the fight than thou that makest the fray.

Music, whilst BASSANIO comments on the caskets to himself

SONG.
    Tell me where is fancy bred,
    Or in the heart, or in the head?
    How begot, how nourished?
    Reply, reply.
    It is engender'd in the eyes,
    With gazing fed; and fancy dies
    In the cradle where it lies.
    Let us all ring fancy's knell
    I'll begin it,--Ding, dong, bell.
ALL
    Ding, dong, bell.
BASSANIO
    So may the outward shows be least themselves:

The world is still deceived with ornament.
In law, what plea so tainted and corrupt,
But, being seasoned with a gracious voice,
Obscures the show of evil? In religion,
What damned error, but some sober brow
Will bless it and approve it with a text,
Hiding the grossness with fair ornament?
There is no vice so simple but assumes
Some mark of virtue on his outward parts:
How many cowards, whose hearts are all as false
As stairs of sand, wear yet upon their chins
The beards of Hercules and frowning Mars;
Who, inward search'd, have livers white as milk;
And these assume but valour's excrement
To render them redoubted! Look on beauty,
And you shall see 'tis purchased by the weight;
Which therein works a miracle in nature,
Making them lightest that wear most of it:
So are those crisped snaky golden locks
Which make such wanton gambols with the wind,
Upon supposed fairness, often known
To be the dowry of a second head,
The skull that bred them in the sepulchre.
Thus ornament is but the guiled shore
To a most dangerous sea; the beauteous scarf
Veiling an Indian beauty; in a word,
The seeming truth which cunning times put on
To entrap the wisest. Therefore, thou gaudy gold,
Hard food for Midas, I will none of thee;
Nor none of thee, thou pale and common drudge
'Tween man and man: but thou, thou meagre lead,
Which rather threatenest than dost promise aught,
Thy paleness moves me more than eloquence;
And here choose I; joy be the consequence!

PORTIA

    [Aside] How all the other passions fleet to air,
    As doubtful thoughts, and rash-embraced despair,
    And shuddering fear, and green-eyed jealousy! O love,
    Be moderate; allay thy ecstasy,
    In measure rein thy joy; scant this excess.
    I feel too much thy blessing: make it less,
    For fear I surfeit.

BASSANIO

    What find I here?

Opening the leaden casket

    Fair Portia's counterfeit! What demi-god
    Hath come so near creation? Move these eyes?
    Or whether, riding on the balls of mine,
    Seem they in motion? Here are sever'd lips,
    Parted with sugar breath: so sweet a bar
    Should sunder such sweet friends. Here in her hairs
    The painter plays the spider and hath woven
    A golden mesh to entrap the hearts of men,
    Faster than gnats in cobwebs; but her eyes,--
    How could he see to do them? having made one,
    Methinks it should have power to steal both his
    And leave itself unfurnish'd. Yet look, how far
    The substance of my praise doth wrong this shadow
    In underprizing it, so far this shadow
    Doth limp behind the substance. Here's the scroll,
    The continent and summary of my fortune.

Reads

    You that choose not by the view,
    Chance as fair and choose as true!
    Since this fortune falls to you,

Be content and seek no new,
If you be well pleased with this
And hold your fortune for your bliss,
Turn you where your lady is
And claim her with a loving kiss.
A gentle scroll. Fair lady, by your leave;
I come by note, to give and to receive.
Like one of two contending in a prize,
That thinks he hath done well in people's eyes,
Hearing applause and universal shout,
Giddy in spirit, still gazing in a doubt
Whether these pearls of praise be his or no;
So, thrice fair lady, stand I, even so;
As doubtful whether what I see be true,
Until confirm'd, sign'd, ratified by you.

PORTIA
You see me, Lord Bassanio, where I stand,
Such as I am: though for myself alone
I would not be ambitious in my wish,
To wish myself much better; yet, for you
I would be trebled twenty times myself;
A thousand times more fair, ten thousand times more
rich;
That only to stand high in your account,
I might in virtue, beauties, livings, friends,
Exceed account; but the full sum of me
Is sum of something, which, to term in gross,
Is an unlesson'd girl, unschool'd, unpractised;
Happy in this, she is not yet so old
But she may learn; happier than this,
She is not bred so dull but she can learn;
Happiest of all is that her gentle spirit
Commits itself to yours to be directed,
As from her lord, her governor, her king.

Myself and what is mine to you and yours
Is now converted: but now I was the lord
Of this fair mansion, master of my servants,
Queen o'er myself: and even now, but now,
This house, these servants and this same myself
Are yours, my lord: I give them with this ring;
Which when you part from, lose, or give away,
Let it presage the ruin of your love
And be my vantage to exclaim on you.

BASSANIO

Madam, you have bereft me of all words,
Only my blood speaks to you in my veins;
And there is such confusion in my powers,
As after some oration fairly spoke
By a beloved prince, there doth appear
Among the buzzing pleased multitude;
Where every something, being blent together,
Turns to a wild of nothing, save of joy,
Express'd and not express'd. But when this ring
Parts from this finger, then parts life from hence:
O, then be bold to say Bassanio's dead!

NERISSA

My lord and lady, it is now our time,
That have stood by and seen our wishes prosper,
To cry, good joy: good joy, my lord and lady!

GRATIANO

My lord Bassanio and my gentle lady,
I wish you all the joy that you can wish;
For I am sure you can wish none from me:
And when your honours mean to solemnize
The bargain of your faith, I do beseech you,
Even at that time I may be married too.

BASSANIO

With all my heart, so thou canst get a wife.

GRATIANO

    I thank your lordship, you have got me one.
    My eyes, my lord, can look as swift as yours:
    You saw the mistress, I beheld the maid;
    You loved, I loved for intermission.
    No more pertains to me, my lord, than you.
    Your fortune stood upon the casket there,
    And so did mine too, as the matter falls;
    For wooing here until I sweat again,
    And sweating until my very roof was dry
    With oaths of love, at last, if promise last,
    I got a promise of this fair one here
    To have her love, provided that your fortune
    Achieved her mistress.

PORTIA

    Is this true, Nerissa?

NERISSA

    Madam, it is, so you stand pleased withal.

BASSANIO

    And do you, Gratiano, mean good faith?

GRATIANO

    Yes, faith, my lord.

BASSANIO

    Our feast shall be much honour'd in your marriage.

GRATIANO

    We'll play with them the first boy for a thousand ducats.

NERISSA

    What, and stake down?

GRATIANO

    No; we shall ne'er win at that sport, and stake down.
    But who comes here? Lorenzo and his infidel? What,
    and my old Venetian friend Salerio?

    Enter LORENZO, JESSICA, and SALERIO, a Messenger
                    from Venice

BASSANIO

    Lorenzo and Salerio, welcome hither;

    If that the youth of my new interest here

    Have power to bid you welcome. By your leave,

    I bid my very friends and countrymen,

    Sweet Portia, welcome.

PORTIA

    So do I, my lord:

    They are entirely welcome.

LORENZO

    I thank your honour. For my part, my lord,

    My purpose was not to have seen you here;

    But meeting with Salerio by the way,

    He did entreat me, past all saying nay,

    To come with him along.

SALERIO

    I did, my lord;

    And I have reason for it. Signior Antonio

    Commends him to you.

Gives Bassanio a letter

BASSANIO

    Ere I ope his letter,

    I pray you, tell me how my good friend doth.

SALERIO

    Not sick, my lord, unless it be in mind;

    Nor well, unless in mind: his letter there

    Will show you his estate.

GRATIANO

    Nerissa, cheer yon stranger; bid her welcome.

    Your hand, Salerio: what's the news from Venice?

    How doth that royal merchant, good Antonio?

    I know he will be glad of our success;

We are the Jasons, we have won the fleece.
SALERIO
I would you had won the fleece that he hath lost.
PORTIA
There are some shrewd contents in yon same paper,
That steals the colour from Bassanio's cheek:
Some dear friend dead; else nothing in the world
Could turn so much the constitution
Of any constant man. What, worse and worse!
With leave, Bassanio: I am half yourself,
And I must freely have the half of anything
That this same paper brings you.
BASSANIO
O sweet Portia,
Here are a few of the unpleasant'st words
That ever blotted paper! Gentle lady,
When I did first impart my love to you,
I freely told you, all the wealth I had
Ran in my veins, I was a gentleman;
And then I told you true: and yet, dear lady,
Rating myself at nothing, you shall see
How much I was a braggart. When I told you
My state was nothing, I should then have told you
That I was worse than nothing; for, indeed,
I have engaged myself to a dear friend,
Engaged my friend to his mere enemy,
To feed my means. Here is a letter, lady;
The paper as the body of my friend,
And every word in it a gaping wound,
Issuing life-blood. But is it true, Salerio?
Have all his ventures fail'd? What, not one hit?
From Tripolis, from Mexico and England,
From Lisbon, Barbary and India?
And not one vessel 'scape the dreadful touch

Of merchant-marring rocks?
SALERIO
　Not one, my lord.
　Besides, it should appear, that if he had
　The present money to discharge the Jew,
　He would not take it. Never did I know
　A creature, that did bear the shape of man,
　So keen and greedy to confound a man:
　He plies the duke at morning and at night,
　And doth impeach the freedom of the state,
　If they deny him justice: twenty merchants,
　The duke himself, and the magnificoes
　Of greatest port, have all persuaded with him;
　But none can drive him from the envious plea
　Of forfeiture, of justice and his bond.
JESSICA
　When I was with him I have heard him swear
　To Tubal and to Chus, his countrymen,
　That he would rather have Antonio's flesh
　Than twenty times the value of the sum
　That he did owe him: and I know, my lord,
　If law, authority and power deny not,
　It will go hard with poor Antonio.
PORTIA
　Is it your dear friend that is thus in trouble?
BASSANIO
　The dearest friend to me, the kindest man,
　The best-condition'd and unwearied spirit
　In doing courtesies, and one in whom
　The ancient Roman honour more appears
　Than any that draws breath in Italy.
PORTIA
　What sum owes he the Jew?
BASSANIO

For me three thousand ducats.

PORTIA

What, no more?
Pay him six thousand, and deface the bond;
Double six thousand, and then treble that,
Before a friend of this description
Shall lose a hair through Bassanio's fault.
First go with me to church and call me wife,
And then away to Venice to your friend;
For never shall you lie by Portia's side
With an unquiet soul. You shall have gold
To pay the petty debt twenty times over:
When it is paid, bring your true friend along.
My maid Nerissa and myself meantime
Will live as maids and widows. Come, away!
For you shall hence upon your wedding-day:
Bid your friends welcome, show a merry cheer:
Since you are dear bought, I will love you dear.
But let me hear the letter of your friend.

BASSANIO

[Reads] Sweet Bassanio, my ships have all
miscarried, my creditors grow cruel, my estate is
very low, my bond to the Jew is forfeit; and since
in paying it, it is impossible I should live, all
debts are cleared between you and I, if I might but
see you at my death. Notwithstanding, use your
pleasure: if your love do not persuade you to come,
let not my letter.

PORTIA

O love, dispatch all business, and be gone!

BASSANIO

Since I have your good leave to go away,
I will make haste: but, till I come again,
No bed shall e'er be guilty of my stay,

No rest be interposer 'twixt us twain.

Exeunt

SCENE III.

Venice. A street.

Enter SHYLOCK, SALARINO, ANTONIO, and Gaoler

SHYLOCK

Gaoler, look to him: tell not me of mercy;
This is the fool that lent out money gratis:
Gaoler, look to him.

ANTONIO

Hear me yet, good Shylock.

SHYLOCK

I'll have my bond; speak not against my bond:
I have sworn an oath that I will have my bond.
Thou call'dst me dog before thou hadst a cause;
But, since I am a dog, beware my fangs:
The duke shall grant me justice. I do wonder,
Thou naughty gaoler, that thou art so fond
To come abroad with him at his request.

ANTONIO

I pray thee, hear me speak.

SHYLOCK

I'll have my bond; I will not hear thee speak:
I'll have my bond; and therefore speak no more.
I'll not be made a soft and dull-eyed fool,
To shake the head, relent, and sigh, and yield
To Christian intercessors. Follow not;
I'll have no speaking: I will have my bond.

Exit

SALARINO

    It is the most impenetrable cur

    That ever kept with men.

ANTONIO

    Let him alone:

    I'll follow him no more with bootless prayers.

    He seeks my life; his reason well I know:

    I oft deliver'd from his forfeitures

    Many that have at times made moan to me;

    Therefore he hates me.

SALARINO

    I am sure the duke

    Will never grant this forfeiture to hold.

ANTONIO

    The duke cannot deny the course of law:

    For the commodity that strangers have

    With us in Venice, if it be denied,

    Will much impeach the justice of his state;

    Since that the trade and profit of the city

    Consisteth of all nations. Therefore, go:

    These griefs and losses have so bated me,

    That I shall hardly spare a pound of flesh

    To-morrow to my bloody creditor.

    Well, gaoler, on. Pray God, Bassanio come

    To see me pay his debt, and then I care not!

Exeunt

SCENE IV.

Belmont. A room in PORTIA'S house.

Enter PORTIA, NERISSA, LORENZO, JESSICA, and BALTHASAR

LORENZO

 Madam, although I speak it in your presence,
 You have a noble and a true conceit
 Of godlike amity; which appears most strongly
 In bearing thus the absence of your lord.
 But if you knew to whom you show this honour,
 How true a gentleman you send relief,
 How dear a lover of my lord your husband,
 I know you would be prouder of the work
 Than customary bounty can enforce you.

PORTIA

 I never did repent for doing good,
 Nor shall not now: for in companions
 That do converse and waste the time together,
 Whose souls do bear an equal yoke Of love,
 There must be needs a like proportion
 Of lineaments, of manners and of spirit;
 Which makes me think that this Antonio,
 Being the bosom lover of my lord,
 Must needs be like my lord. If it be so,
 How little is the cost I have bestow'd
 In purchasing the semblance of my soul
 From out the state of hellish misery!
 This comes too near the praising of myself;
 Therefore no more of it: hear other things.
 Lorenzo, I commit into your hands
 The husbandry and manage of my house
 Until my lord's return: for mine own part,
 I have toward heaven breathed a secret vow

To live in prayer and contemplation,
Only attended by Nerissa here,
Until her husband and my lord's return:
There is a monastery two miles off;
And there will we abide. I do desire you
Not to deny this imposition;
The which my love and some necessity
Now lays upon you.

LORENZO
Madam, with all my heart;
I shall obey you in all fair commands.

PORTIA
My people do already know my mind,
And will acknowledge you and Jessica
In place of Lord Bassanio and myself.
And so farewell, till we shall meet again.

LORENZO
Fair thoughts and happy hours attend on you!

JESSICA
I wish your ladyship all heart's content.

PORTIA
I thank you for your wish, and am well pleased
To wish it back on you: fare you well Jessica.

Exeunt JESSICA and LORENZO

Now, Balthasar,
As I have ever found thee honest-true,
So let me find thee still. Take this same letter,
And use thou all the endeavour of a man
In speed to Padua: see thou render this
Into my cousin's hand, Doctor Bellario;
And, look, what notes and garments he doth give thee,
Bring them, I pray thee, with imagined speed
Unto the tranect, to the common ferry

Which trades to Venice. Waste no time in words,
But get thee gone: I shall be there before thee.
BALTHASAR
Madam, I go with all convenient speed.

Exit

PORTIA
Come on, Nerissa; I have work in hand
That you yet know not of: we'll see our husbands
Before they think of us.
NERISSA
Shall they see us?
PORTIA
They shall, Nerissa; but in such a habit,
That they shall think we are accomplished
With that we lack. I'll hold thee any wager,
When we are both accoutred like young men,
I'll prove the prettier fellow of the two,
And wear my dagger with the braver grace,
And speak between the change of man and boy
With a reed voice, and turn two mincing steps
Into a manly stride, and speak of frays
Like a fine bragging youth, and tell quaint lies,
How honourable ladies sought my love,
Which I denying, they fell sick and died;
I could not do withal; then I'll repent,
And wish for all that, that I had not killed them;
And twenty of these puny lies I'll tell,
That men shall swear I have discontinued school
Above a twelvemonth. I have within my mind
A thousand raw tricks of these bragging Jacks,
Which I will practise.
NERISSA
Why, shall we turn to men?

PORTIA

Fie, what a question's that,
If thou wert near a lewd interpreter!
But come, I'll tell thee all my whole device
When I am in my coach, which stays for us
At the park gate; and therefore haste away,
For we must measure twenty miles to-day.

Exeunt

SCENE V.

The same. A garden.

Enter LAUNCELOT and JESSICA

LAUNCELOT

Yes, truly; for, look you, the sins of the father
are to be laid upon the children: therefore, I
promise ye, I fear you. I was always plain with
you, and so now I speak my agitation of the matter:
therefore be of good cheer, for truly I think you
are damned. There is but one hope in it that can do
you any good; and that is but a kind of bastard
hope neither.

JESSICA

And what hope is that, I pray thee?

LAUNCELOT

Marry, you may partly hope that your father got you
not, that you are not the Jew's daughter.

JESSICA

That were a kind of bastard hope, indeed: so the
sins of my mother should be visited upon me.

LAUNCELOT

Truly then I fear you are damned both by father and
mother: thus when I shun Scylla, your father, I

fall into Charybdis, your mother: well, you are
gone both ways.

JESSICA

I shall be saved by my husband; he hath made me a
Christian.

LAUNCELOT

Truly, the more to blame he: we were Christians
enow before; e'en as many as could well live, one by
another. This making Christians will raise the
price of hogs: if we grow all to be pork-eaters, we
shall not shortly have a rasher on the coals for money.

Enter LORENZO

JESSICA

I'll tell my husband, Launcelot, what you say: here he
comes.

LORENZO

I shall grow jealous of you shortly, Launcelot, if
you thus get my wife into corners.

JESSICA

Nay, you need not fear us, Lorenzo: Launcelot and I
are out. He tells me flatly, there is no mercy for
me in heaven, because I am a Jew's daughter: and he
says, you are no good member of the commonwealth,
for in converting Jews to Christians, you raise the
price of pork.

LORENZO

I shall answer that better to the commonwealth than
you can the getting up of the negro's belly: the
Moor is with child by you, Launcelot.

LAUNCELOT

It is much that the Moor should be more than reason:
but if she be less than an honest woman, she is
indeed more than I took her for.

LORENZO

How every fool can play upon the word! I think the
best grace of wit will shortly turn into silence,
and discourse grow commendable in none only but
parrots. Go in, sirrah; bid them prepare for dinner.

LAUNCELOT

That is done, sir; they have all stomachs.

LORENZO

Goodly Lord, what a wit-snapper are you! then bid
them prepare dinner.

LAUNCELOT

That is done too, sir; only 'cover' is the word.

LORENZO

Will you cover then, sir?

LAUNCELOT

Not so, sir, neither; I know my duty.

LORENZO

Yet more quarrelling with occasion! Wilt thou show
the whole wealth of thy wit in an instant? I pray
tree, understand a plain man in his plain meaning:
go to thy fellows; bid them cover the table, serve
in the meat, and we will come in to dinner.

LAUNCELOT

For the table, sir, it shall be served in; for the
meat, sir, it shall be covered; for your coming in
to dinner, sir, why, let it be as humours and
conceits shall govern.

Exit

LORENZO

O dear discretion, how his words are suited!
The fool hath planted in his memory
An army of good words; and I do know
A many fools, that stand in better place,

Garnish'd like him, that for a tricksy word
Defy the matter. How cheerest thou, Jessica?
And now, good sweet, say thy opinion,
How dost thou like the Lord Bassanio's wife?
JESSICA
Past all expressing. It is very meet
The Lord Bassanio live an upright life;
For, having such a blessing in his lady,
He finds the joys of heaven here on earth;
And if on earth he do not mean it, then
In reason he should never come to heaven
Why, if two gods should play some heavenly match
And on the wager lay two earthly women,
And Portia one, there must be something else
Pawn'd with the other, for the poor rude world
Hath not her fellow.
LORENZO
Even such a husband
Hast thou of me as she is for a wife.
JESSICA
Nay, but ask my opinion too of that.
LORENZO
I will anon: first, let us go to dinner.
JESSICA
Nay, let me praise you while I have a stomach.
LORENZO
No, pray thee, let it serve for table-talk;
Then, howso'er thou speak'st, 'mong other things
I shall digest it.
JESSICA
Well, I'll set you forth.

Exeunt

ACT IV

SCENE I.

Venice. A court of justice.

Enter the DUKE, the Magnificoes, ANTONIO, BASSANIO, GRATIANO, SALERIO, and others

DUKE
  What, is Antonio here?
ANTONIO
  Ready, so please your grace.
DUKE
  I am sorry for thee: thou art come to answer
  A stony adversary, an inhuman wretch
  uncapable of pity, void and empty
  From any dram of mercy.
ANTONIO
  I have heard
  Your grace hath ta'en great pains to qualify
  His rigorous course; but since he stands obdurate
  And that no lawful means can carry me
  Out of his envy's reach, I do oppose
  My patience to his fury, and am arm'd
  To suffer, with a quietness of spirit,
  The very tyranny and rage of his.
DUKE
  Go one, and call the Jew into the court.
SALERIO
  He is ready at the door: he comes, my lord.

Enter SHYLOCK

DUKE

Make room, and let him stand before our face.
Shylock, the world thinks, and I think so too,
That thou but lead'st this fashion of thy malice
To the last hour of act; and then 'tis thought
Thou'lt show thy mercy and remorse more strange
Than is thy strange apparent cruelty;
And where thou now exact'st the penalty,
Which is a pound of this poor merchant's flesh,
Thou wilt not only loose the forfeiture,
But, touch'd with human gentleness and love,
Forgive a moiety of the principal;
Glancing an eye of pity on his losses,
That have of late so huddled on his back,
Enow to press a royal merchant down
And pluck commiseration of his state
From brassy bosoms and rough hearts of flint,
From stubborn Turks and Tartars, never train'd
To offices of tender courtesy.
We all expect a gentle answer, Jew.

SHYLOCK

I have possess'd your grace of what I purpose;
And by our holy Sabbath have I sworn
To have the due and forfeit of my bond:
If you deny it, let the danger light
Upon your charter and your city's freedom.
You'll ask me, why I rather choose to have
A weight of carrion flesh than to receive
Three thousand ducats: I'll not answer that:
But, say, it is my humour: is it answer'd?
What if my house be troubled with a rat
And I be pleased to give ten thousand ducats
To have it baned? What, are you answer'd yet?
Some men there are love not a gaping pig;
Some, that are mad if they behold a cat;

And others, when the bagpipe sings i' the nose,
Cannot contain their urine: for affection,
Mistress of passion, sways it to the mood
Of what it likes or loathes. Now, for your answer:
As there is no firm reason to be render'd,
Why he cannot abide a gaping pig;
Why he, a harmless necessary cat;
Why he, a woollen bagpipe; but of force
Must yield to such inevitable shame
As to offend, himself being offended;
So can I give no reason, nor I will not,
More than a lodged hate and a certain loathing
I bear Antonio, that I follow thus
A losing suit against him. Are you answer'd?

BASSANIO

This is no answer, thou unfeeling man,
To excuse the current of thy cruelty.

SHYLOCK

I am not bound to please thee with my answers.

BASSANIO

Do all men kill the things they do not love?

SHYLOCK

Hates any man the thing he would not kill?

BASSANIO

Every offence is not a hate at first.

SHYLOCK

What, wouldst thou have a serpent sting thee twice?

ANTONIO

I pray you, think you question with the Jew:
You may as well go stand upon the beach
And bid the main flood bate his usual height;
You may as well use question with the wolf
Why he hath made the ewe bleat for the lamb;
You may as well forbid the mountain pines

To wag their high tops and to make no noise,
When they are fretten with the gusts of heaven;
You may as well do anything most hard,
As seek to soften that--than which what's harder?--
His Jewish heart: therefore, I do beseech you,
Make no more offers, use no farther means,
But with all brief and plain conveniency
Let me have judgment and the Jew his will.

BASSANIO

For thy three thousand ducats here is six.

SHYLOCK

What judgment shall I dread, doing
Were in six parts and every part a ducat,
I would not draw them; I would have my bond.

DUKE

How shalt thou hope for mercy, rendering none?

SHYLOCK

What judgment shall I dread, doing no wrong?
You have among you many a purchased slave,
Which, like your asses and your dogs and mules,
You use in abject and in slavish parts,
Because you bought them: shall I say to you,
Let them be free, marry them to your heirs?
Why sweat they under burthens? let their beds
Be made as soft as yours and let their palates
Be season'd with such viands? You will answer
'The slaves are ours:' so do I answer you:
The pound of flesh, which I demand of him,
Is dearly bought; 'tis mine and I will have it.
If you deny me, fie upon your law!
There is no force in the decrees of Venice.
I stand for judgment: answer; shall I have it?

DUKE

Upon my power I may dismiss this court,

Unless Bellario, a learned doctor,
Whom I have sent for to determine this,
Come here to-day.
SALERIO
My lord, here stays without
A messenger with letters from the doctor,
New come from Padua.
DUKE
Bring us the letter; call the messenger.
BASSANIO
Good cheer, Antonio! What, man, courage yet!
The Jew shall have my flesh, blood, bones and all,
Ere thou shalt lose for me one drop of blood.
ANTONIO
I am a tainted wether of the flock,
Meetest for death: the weakest kind of fruit
Drops earliest to the ground; and so let me
You cannot better be employ'd, Bassanio,
Than to live still and write mine epitaph.

Enter NERISSA, dressed like a lawyer's clerk

DUKE
Came you from Padua, from Bellario?
NERISSA
From both, my lord. Bellario greets your grace.

Presenting a letter

BASSANIO
Why dost thou whet thy knife so earnestly?
SHYLOCK
To cut the forfeiture from that bankrupt there.
GRATIANO
Not on thy sole, but on thy soul, harsh Jew,

Thou makest thy knife keen; but no metal can,
No, not the hangman's axe, bear half the keenness
Of thy sharp envy. Can no prayers pierce thee?
SHYLOCK
No, none that thou hast wit enough to make.
GRATIANO
O, be thou damn'd, inexecrable dog!
And for thy life let justice be accused.
Thou almost makest me waver in my faith
To hold opinion with Pythagoras,
That souls of animals infuse themselves
Into the trunks of men: thy currish spirit
Govern'd a wolf, who, hang'd for human slaughter,
Even from the gallows did his fell soul fleet,
And, whilst thou lay'st in thy unhallow'd dam,
Infused itself in thee; for thy desires
Are wolvish, bloody, starved and ravenous.
SHYLOCK
Till thou canst rail the seal from off my bond,
Thou but offend'st thy lungs to speak so loud:
Repair thy wit, good youth, or it will fall
To cureless ruin. I stand here for law.
DUKE
This letter from Bellario doth commend
A young and learned doctor to our court.
Where is he?
NERISSA
He attendeth here hard by,
To know your answer, whether you'll admit him.
DUKE
With all my heart. Some three or four of you
Go give him courteous conduct to this place.
Meantime the court shall hear Bellario's letter.
Clerk

[Reads]

Your grace shall understand that at the receipt of
your letter I am very sick: but in the instant that
your messenger came, in loving visitation was with
me a young doctor of Rome; his name is Balthasar. I
acquainted him with the cause in controversy between
the Jew and Antonio the merchant: we turned o'er
many books together: he is furnished with my
opinion; which, bettered with his own learning, the
greatness whereof I cannot enough commend, comes
with him, at my importunity, to fill up your grace's
request in my stead. I beseech you, let his lack of
years be no impediment to let him lack a reverend
estimation; for I never knew so young a body with so
old a head. I leave him to your gracious
acceptance, whose trial shall better publish his
commendation.

DUKE

You hear the learn'd Bellario, what he writes:
And here, I take it, is the doctor come.

Enter PORTIA, dressed like a doctor of laws

Give me your hand. Come you from old Bellario?

PORTIA

I did, my lord.

DUKE

You are welcome: take your place.
Are you acquainted with the difference
That holds this present question in the court?

PORTIA

I am informed thoroughly of the cause.
Which is the merchant here, and which the Jew?

DUKE

Antonio and old Shylock, both stand forth.

PORTIA
  Is your name Shylock?
SHYLOCK
  Shylock is my name.
PORTIA
  Of a strange nature is the suit you follow;
  Yet in such rule that the Venetian law
  Cannot impugn you as you do proceed.
  You stand within his danger, do you not?
ANTONIO
  Ay, so he says.
PORTIA
  Do you confess the bond?
ANTONIO
  I do.
PORTIA
  Then must the Jew be merciful.
SHYLOCK
  On what compulsion must I? tell me that.
PORTIA
  The quality of mercy is not strain'd,
  It droppeth as the gentle rain from heaven
  Upon the place beneath: it is twice blest;
  It blesseth him that gives and him that takes:
  'Tis mightiest in the mightiest: it becomes
  The throned monarch better than his crown;
  His sceptre shows the force of temporal power,
  The attribute to awe and majesty,
  Wherein doth sit the dread and fear of kings;
  But mercy is above this sceptred sway;
  It is enthroned in the hearts of kings,
  It is an attribute to God himself;
  And earthly power doth then show likest God's
  When mercy seasons justice. Therefore, Jew,

Though justice be thy plea, consider this,
That, in the course of justice, none of us
Should see salvation: we do pray for mercy;
And that same prayer doth teach us all to render
The deeds of mercy. I have spoke thus much
To mitigate the justice of thy plea;
Which if thou follow, this strict court of Venice
Must needs give sentence 'gainst the merchant there.

SHYLOCK

My deeds upon my head! I crave the law,
The penalty and forfeit of my bond.

PORTIA

Is he not able to discharge the money?

BASSANIO

Yes, here I tender it for him in the court;
Yea, twice the sum: if that will not suffice,
I will be bound to pay it ten times o'er,
On forfeit of my hands, my head, my heart:
If this will not suffice, it must appear
That malice bears down truth. And I beseech you,
Wrest once the law to your authority:
To do a great right, do a little wrong,
And curb this cruel devil of his will.

PORTIA

It must not be; there is no power in Venice
Can alter a decree established:
'Twill be recorded for a precedent,
And many an error by the same example
Will rush into the state: it cannot be.

SHYLOCK

A Daniel come to judgment! yea, a Daniel!
O wise young judge, how I do honour thee!

PORTIA

I pray you, let me look upon the bond.

SHYLOCK

Here 'tis, most reverend doctor, here it is.

PORTIA

Shylock, there's thrice thy money offer'd thee.

SHYLOCK

An oath, an oath, I have an oath in heaven:
Shall I lay perjury upon my soul?
No, not for Venice.

PORTIA

Why, this bond is forfeit;
And lawfully by this the Jew may claim
A pound of flesh, to be by him cut off
Nearest the merchant's heart. Be merciful:
Take thrice thy money; bid me tear the bond.

SHYLOCK

When it is paid according to the tenor.
It doth appear you are a worthy judge;
You know the law, your exposition
Hath been most sound: I charge you by the law,
Whereof you are a well-deserving pillar,
Proceed to judgment: by my soul I swear
There is no power in the tongue of man
To alter me: I stay here on my bond.

ANTONIO

Most heartily I do beseech the court
To give the judgment.

PORTIA

Why then, thus it is:
You must prepare your bosom for his knife.

SHYLOCK

O noble judge! O excellent young man!

PORTIA

For the intent and purpose of the law
Hath full relation to the penalty,

Which here appeareth due upon the bond.

SHYLOCK

'Tis very true: O wise and upright judge!
How much more elder art thou than thy looks!

PORTIA

Therefore lay bare your bosom.

SHYLOCK

Ay, his breast:
So says the bond: doth it not, noble judge?
'Nearest his heart:' those are the very words.

PORTIA

It is so. Are there balance here to weigh
The flesh?

SHYLOCK

I have them ready.

PORTIA

Have by some surgeon, Shylock, on your charge,
To stop his wounds, lest he do bleed to death.

SHYLOCK

Is it so nominated in the bond?

PORTIA

It is not so express'd: but what of that?
'Twere good you do so much for charity.

SHYLOCK

I cannot find it; 'tis not in the bond.

PORTIA

You, merchant, have you any thing to say?

ANTONIO

But little: I am arm'd and well prepared.
Give me your hand, Bassanio: fare you well!
Grieve not that I am fallen to this for you;
For herein Fortune shows herself more kind
Than is her custom: it is still her use
To let the wretched man outlive his wealth,

To view with hollow eye and wrinkled brow
An age of poverty; from which lingering penance
Of such misery doth she cut me off.
Commend me to your honourable wife:
Tell her the process of Antonio's end;
Say how I loved you, speak me fair in death;
And, when the tale is told, bid her be judge
Whether Bassanio had not once a love.
Repent but you that you shall lose your friend,
And he repents not that he pays your debt;
For if the Jew do cut but deep enough,
I'll pay it presently with all my heart.

BASSANIO

Antonio, I am married to a wife
Which is as dear to me as life itself;
But life itself, my wife, and all the world,
Are not with me esteem'd above thy life:
I would lose all, ay, sacrifice them all
Here to this devil, to deliver you.

PORTIA

Your wife would give you little thanks for that,
If she were by, to hear you make the offer.

GRATIANO

I have a wife, whom, I protest, I love:
I would she were in heaven, so she could
Entreat some power to change this currish Jew.

NERISSA

'Tis well you offer it behind her back;
The wish would make else an unquiet house.

SHYLOCK

These be the Christian husbands. I have a daughter;
Would any of the stock of Barrabas
Had been her husband rather than a Christian!

Aside

92

We trifle time: I pray thee, pursue sentence.
PORTIA

A pound of that same merchant's flesh is thine:
The court awards it, and the law doth give it.
SHYLOCK

Most rightful judge!
PORTIA

And you must cut this flesh from off his breast:
The law allows it, and the court awards it.
SHYLOCK

Most learned judge! A sentence! Come, prepare!
PORTIA

Tarry a little; there is something else.
This bond doth give thee here no jot of blood;
The words expressly are 'a pound of flesh:'
Take then thy bond, take thou thy pound of flesh;
But, in the cutting it, if thou dost shed
One drop of Christian blood, thy lands and goods
Are, by the laws of Venice, confiscate
Unto the state of Venice.
GRATIANO

O upright judge! Mark, Jew: O learned judge!
SHYLOCK

Is that the law?
PORTIA

Thyself shalt see the act:
For, as thou urgest justice, be assured
Thou shalt have justice, more than thou desirest.
GRATIANO

O learned judge! Mark, Jew: a learned judge!
SHYLOCK

I take this offer, then; pay the bond thrice
And let the Christian go.

BASSANIO

Here is the money.

PORTIA

Soft!

The Jew shall have all justice; soft! no haste:

He shall have nothing but the penalty.

GRATIANO

O Jew! an upright judge, a learned judge!

PORTIA

Therefore prepare thee to cut off the flesh.

Shed thou no blood, nor cut thou less nor more

But just a pound of flesh: if thou cut'st more

Or less than a just pound, be it but so much

As makes it light or heavy in the substance,

Or the division of the twentieth part

Of one poor scruple, nay, if the scale do turn

But in the estimation of a hair,

Thou diest and all thy goods are confiscate.

GRATIANO

A second Daniel, a Daniel, Jew!

Now, infidel, I have you on the hip.

PORTIA

Why doth the Jew pause? take thy forfeiture.

SHYLOCK

Give me my principal, and let me go.

BASSANIO

I have it ready for thee; here it is.

PORTIA

He hath refused it in the open court:

He shall have merely justice and his bond.

GRATIANO

A Daniel, still say I, a second Daniel!

I thank thee, Jew, for teaching me that word.

SHYLOCK

Shall I not have barely my principal?
PORTIA
Thou shalt have nothing but the forfeiture,
To be so taken at thy peril, Jew.
SHYLOCK
Why, then the devil give him good of it!
I'll stay no longer question.
PORTIA
Tarry, Jew:
The law hath yet another hold on you.
It is enacted in the laws of Venice,
If it be proved against an alien
That by direct or indirect attempts
He seek the life of any citizen,
The party 'gainst the which he doth contrive
Shall seize one half his goods; the other half
Comes to the privy coffer of the state;
And the offender's life lies in the mercy
Of the duke only, 'gainst all other voice.
In which predicament, I say, thou stand'st;
For it appears, by manifest proceeding,
That indirectly and directly too
Thou hast contrived against the very life
Of the defendant; and thou hast incurr'd
The danger formerly by me rehearsed.
Down therefore and beg mercy of the duke.
GRATIANO
Beg that thou mayst have leave to hang thyself:
And yet, thy wealth being forfeit to the state,
Thou hast not left the value of a cord;
Therefore thou must be hang'd at the state's charge.
DUKE
That thou shalt see the difference of our spirits,
I pardon thee thy life before thou ask it:

For half thy wealth, it is Antonio's;
The other half comes to the general state,
Which humbleness may drive unto a fine.

PORTIA

Ay, for the state, not for Antonio.

SHYLOCK

Nay, take my life and all; pardon not that:
You take my house when you do take the prop
That doth sustain my house; you take my life
When you do take the means whereby I live.

PORTIA

What mercy can you render him, Antonio?

GRATIANO

A halter gratis; nothing else, for God's sake.

ANTONIO

So please my lord the duke and all the court
To quit the fine for one half of his goods,
I am content; so he will let me have
The other half in use, to render it,
Upon his death, unto the gentleman
That lately stole his daughter:
Two things provided more, that, for this favour,
He presently become a Christian;
The other, that he do record a gift,
Here in the court, of all he dies possess'd,
Unto his son Lorenzo and his daughter.

DUKE

He shall do this, or else I do recant
The pardon that I late pronounced here.

PORTIA

Art thou contented, Jew? what dost thou say?

SHYLOCK

I am content.

PORTIA

Clerk, draw a deed of gift.

SHYLOCK

I pray you, give me leave to go from hence;
I am not well: send the deed after me,
And I will sign it.

DUKE

Get thee gone, but do it.

GRATIANO

In christening shalt thou have two god-fathers:
Had I been judge, thou shouldst have had ten more,
To bring thee to the gallows, not the font.

Exit SHYLOCK

DUKE

Sir, I entreat you home with me to dinner.

PORTIA

I humbly do desire your grace of pardon:
I must away this night toward Padua,
And it is meet I presently set forth.

DUKE

I am sorry that your leisure serves you not.
Antonio, gratify this gentleman,
For, in my mind, you are much bound to him.

Exeunt Duke and his train

BASSANIO

Most worthy gentleman, I and my friend
Have by your wisdom been this day acquitted
Of grievous penalties; in lieu whereof,
Three thousand ducats, due unto the Jew,
We freely cope your courteous pains withal.

ANTONIO

And stand indebted, over and above,

In love and service to you evermore.
PORTIA
    He is well paid that is well satisfied;
    And I, delivering you, am satisfied
    And therein do account myself well paid:
    My mind was never yet more mercenary.
    I pray you, know me when we meet again:
    I wish you well, and so I take my leave.
BASSANIO
    Dear sir, of force I must attempt you further:
    Take some remembrance of us, as a tribute,
    Not as a fee: grant me two things, I pray you,
    Not to deny me, and to pardon me.
PORTIA
    You press me far, and therefore I will yield.

To ANTONIO

Give me your gloves, I'll wear them for your sake;

To BASSANIO

    And, for your love, I'll take this ring from you:
    Do not draw back your hand; I'll take no more;
    And you in love shall not deny me this.
BASSANIO
    This ring, good sir, alas, it is a trifle!
    I will not shame myself to give you this.
PORTIA
    I will have nothing else but only this;
    And now methinks I have a mind to it.
BASSANIO
    There's more depends on this than on the value.
    The dearest ring in Venice will I give you,
    And find it out by proclamation:

Only for this, I pray you, pardon me.

PORTIA

I see, sir, you are liberal in offers

You taught me first to beg; and now methinks

You teach me how a beggar should be answer'd.

BASSANIO

Good sir, this ring was given me by my wife;

And when she put it on, she made me vow

That I should neither sell nor give nor lose it.

PORTIA

That 'scuse serves many men to save their gifts.

An if your wife be not a mad-woman,

And know how well I have deserved the ring,

She would not hold out enemy for ever,

For giving it to me. Well, peace be with you!

Exeunt Portia and Nerissa

ANTONIO

My Lord Bassanio, let him have the ring:

Let his deservings and my love withal

Be valued against your wife's commandment.

BASSANIO

Go, Gratiano, run and overtake him;

Give him the ring, and bring him, if thou canst,

Unto Antonio's house: away! make haste.

Exit Gratiano

Come, you and I will thither presently;

And in the morning early will we both

Fly toward Belmont: come, Antonio.

Exeunt

SCENE II.

The same. A street.

Enter PORTIA and NERISSA

PORTIA

    Inquire the Jew's house out, give him this deed
    And let him sign it: we'll away to-night
    And be a day before our husbands home:
    This deed will be well welcome to Lorenzo.

Enter GRATIANO

GRATIANO

    Fair sir, you are well o'erta'en
    My Lord Bassanio upon more advice
    Hath sent you here this ring, and doth entreat
    Your company at dinner.

PORTIA

    That cannot be:
    His ring I do accept most thankfully:
    And so, I pray you, tell him: furthermore,
    I pray you, show my youth old Shylock's house.

GRATIANO

    That will I do.

NERISSA

    Sir, I would speak with you.

Aside to PORTIA

    I'll see if I can get my husband's ring,
    Which I did make him swear to keep for ever.

PORTIA

    [Aside to NERISSA] Thou mayst, I warrant.
    We shall have old swearing
    That they did give the rings away to men;

But we'll outface them, and outswear them too.

Aloud

Away! make haste: thou knowist where I will tarry.
NERISSA
Come, good sir, will you show me to this house?

Exeunt

ACT V

SCENE I.

Belmont. Avenue to PORTIA'S house.

Enter LORENZO and JESSICA

LORENZO
>The moon shines bright: in such a night as this,
>When the sweet wind did gently kiss the trees
>And they did make no noise, in such a night
>Troilus methinks mounted the Troyan walls
>And sigh'd his soul toward the Grecian tents,
>Where Cressid lay that night.

JESSICA
>In such a night
>Did Thisbe fearfully o'ertrip the dew
>And saw the lion's shadow ere himself
>And ran dismay'd away.

LORENZO
>In such a night
>Stood Dido with a willow in her hand
>Upon the wild sea banks and waft her love
>To come again to Carthage.

JESSICA
>In such a night
>Medea gather'd the enchanted herbs
>That did renew old AEson.

LORENZO
>In such a night
>Did Jessica steal from the wealthy Jew
>And with an unthrift love did run from Venice
>As far as Belmont.

JESSICA

In such a night
Did young Lorenzo swear he loved her well,
Stealing her soul with many vows of faith
And ne'er a true one.
LORENZO
In such a night
Did pretty Jessica, like a little shrew,
Slander her love, and he forgave it her.
JESSICA
I would out-night you, did no body come;
But, hark, I hear the footing of a man.

Enter STEPHANO

LORENZO
Who comes so fast in silence of the night?
STEPHANO
A friend.
LORENZO
A friend! what friend? your name, I pray you, friend?
STEPHANO
Stephano is my name; and I bring word
My mistress will before the break of day
Be here at Belmont; she doth stray about
By holy crosses, where she kneels and prays
For happy wedlock hours.
LORENZO
Who comes with her?
STEPHANO
None but a holy hermit and her maid.
I pray you, is my master yet return'd?
LORENZO
He is not, nor we have not heard from him.
But go we in, I pray thee, Jessica,
And ceremoniously let us prepare

Some welcome for the mistress of the house.

Enter LAUNCELOT

LAUNCELOT
Sola, sola! wo ha, ho! sola, sola!
LORENZO
Who calls?
LAUNCELOT
Sola! did you see Master Lorenzo?
Master Lorenzo, sola, sola!
LORENZO
Leave hollaing, man: here.
LAUNCELOT
Sola! where? where?
LORENZO
Here.
LAUNCELOT
Tell him there's a post come from my master, with
his horn full of good news: my master will be here
ere morning.

Exit

LORENZO
Sweet soul, let's in, and there expect their coming.
And yet no matter: why should we go in?
My friend Stephano, signify, I pray you,
Within the house, your mistress is at hand;
And bring your music forth into the air.

Exit Stephano

How sweet the moonlight sleeps upon this bank!
Here will we sit and let the sounds of music
Creep in our ears: soft stillness and the night

Become the touches of sweet harmony.
Sit, Jessica. Look how the floor of heaven
Is thick inlaid with patines of bright gold:
There's not the smallest orb which thou behold'st
But in his motion like an angel sings,
Still quiring to the young-eyed cherubins;
Such harmony is in immortal souls;
But whilst this muddy vesture of decay
Doth grossly close it in, we cannot hear it.

Enter Musicians

Come, ho! and wake Diana with a hymn!
With sweetest touches pierce your mistress' ear,
And draw her home with music.

Music

JESSICA
    I am never merry when I hear sweet music.
LORENZO
    The reason is, your spirits are attentive:
For do but note a wild and wanton herd,
Or race of youthful and unhandled colts,
Fetching mad bounds, bellowing and neighing loud,
Which is the hot condition of their blood;
If they but hear perchance a trumpet sound,
Or any air of music touch their ears,
You shall perceive them make a mutual stand,
Their savage eyes turn'd to a modest gaze
By the sweet power of music: therefore the poet
Did feign that Orpheus drew trees, stones and floods;
Since nought so stockish, hard and full of rage,
But music for the time doth change his nature.
The man that hath no music in himself,

Nor is not moved with concord of sweet sounds,
Is fit for treasons, stratagems and spoils;
The motions of his spirit are dull as night
And his affections dark as Erebus:
Let no such man be trusted. Mark the music.

Enter PORTIA and NERISSA

PORTIA

That light we see is burning in my hall.
How far that little candle throws his beams!
So shines a good deed in a naughty world.

NERISSA

When the moon shone, we did not see the candle.

PORTIA

So doth the greater glory dim the less:
A substitute shines brightly as a king
Unto the king be by, and then his state
Empties itself, as doth an inland brook
Into the main of waters. Music! hark!

NERISSA

It is your music, madam, of the house.

PORTIA

Nothing is good, I see, without respect:
Methinks it sounds much sweeter than by day.

NERISSA

Silence bestows that virtue on it, madam.

PORTIA

The crow doth sing as sweetly as the lark,
When neither is attended, and I think
The nightingale, if she should sing by day,
When every goose is cackling, would be thought
No better a musician than the wren.
How many things by season season'd are
To their right praise and true perfection!

Peace, ho! the moon sleeps with Endymion
And would not be awaked.

Music ceases

LORENZO

That is the voice,
Or I am much deceived, of Portia.

PORTIA

He knows me as the blind man knows the cuckoo,
By the bad voice.

LORENZO

Dear lady, welcome home.

PORTIA

We have been praying for our husbands' healths,
Which speed, we hope, the better for our words.
Are they return'd?

LORENZO

Madam, they are not yet;
But there is come a messenger before,
To signify their coming.

PORTIA

Go in, Nerissa;
Give order to my servants that they take
No note at all of our being absent hence;
Nor you, Lorenzo; Jessica, nor you.

A tucket sounds

LORENZO

Your husband is at hand; I hear his trumpet:
We are no tell-tales, madam; fear you not.

PORTIA

This night methinks is but the daylight sick;
It looks a little paler: 'tis a day,

Such as the day is when the sun is hid.

Enter BASSANIO, ANTONIO, GRATIANO, and their
followers

BASSANIO
　　We should hold day with the Antipodes,
　　If you would walk in absence of the sun.
PORTIA
　　Let me give light, but let me not be light;
　　For a light wife doth make a heavy husband,
　　And never be Bassanio so for me:
　　But God sort all! You are welcome home, my lord.
BASSANIO
　　I thank you, madam. Give welcome to my friend.
　　This is the man, this is Antonio,
　　To whom I am so infinitely bound.
PORTIA
　　You should in all sense be much bound to him.
　　For, as I hear, he was much bound for you.
ANTONIO
　　No more than I am well acquitted of.
PORTIA
　　Sir, you are very welcome to our house:
　　It must appear in other ways than words,
　　Therefore I scant this breathing courtesy.
GRATIANO
[To NERISSA] By yonder moon I swear you do me wrong;
　　In faith, I gave it to the judge's clerk:
　　Would he were gelt that had it, for my part,
　　Since you do take it, love, so much at heart.
PORTIA
　　A quarrel, ho, already! what's the matter?
GRATIANO

About a hoop of gold, a paltry ring
That she did give me, whose posy was
For all the world like cutler's poetry
Upon a knife, 'Love me, and leave me not.'

NERISSA

What talk you of the posy or the value?
You swore to me, when I did give it you,
That you would wear it till your hour of death
And that it should lie with you in your grave:
Though not for me, yet for your vehement oaths,
You should have been respective and have kept it.
Gave it a judge's clerk! no, God's my judge,
The clerk will ne'er wear hair on's face that had it.

GRATIANO

He will, an if he live to be a man.

NERISSA

Ay, if a woman live to be a man.

GRATIANO

Now, by this hand, I gave it to a youth,
A kind of boy, a little scrubbed boy,
No higher than thyself; the judge's clerk,
A prating boy, that begg'd it as a fee:
I could not for my heart deny it him.

PORTIA

You were to blame, I must be plain with you,
To part so slightly with your wife's first gift:
A thing stuck on with oaths upon your finger
And so riveted with faith unto your flesh.
I gave my love a ring and made him swear
Never to part with it; and here he stands;
I dare be sworn for him he would not leave it
Nor pluck it from his finger, for the wealth
That the world masters. Now, in faith, Gratiano,
You give your wife too unkind a cause of grief:

An 'twere to me, I should be mad at it.
BASSANIO

[Aside] Why, I were best to cut my left hand off
And swear I lost the ring defending it.
GRATIANO

My Lord Bassanio gave his ring away
Unto the judge that begg'd it and indeed
Deserved it too; and then the boy, his clerk,
That took some pains in writing, he begg'd mine;
And neither man nor master would take aught
But the two rings.
PORTIA

What ring gave you my lord?
Not that, I hope, which you received of me.
BASSANIO

If I could add a lie unto a fault,
I would deny it; but you see my finger
Hath not the ring upon it; it is gone.
PORTIA

Even so void is your false heart of truth.
By heaven, I will ne'er come in your bed
Until I see the ring.
NERISSA

Nor I in yours
Till I again see mine.
BASSANIO

Sweet Portia,
If you did know to whom I gave the ring,
If you did know for whom I gave the ring
And would conceive for what I gave the ring
And how unwillingly I left the ring,
When nought would be accepted but the ring,
You would abate the strength of your displeasure.
PORTIA

If you had known the virtue of the ring,
Or half her worthiness that gave the ring,
Or your own honour to contain the ring,
You would not then have parted with the ring.
What man is there so much unreasonable,
If you had pleased to have defended it
With any terms of zeal, wanted the modesty
To urge the thing held as a ceremony?
Nerissa teaches me what to believe:
I'll die for't but some woman had the ring.

BASSANIO

No, by my honour, madam, by my soul,
No woman had it, but a civil doctor,
Which did refuse three thousand ducats of me
And begg'd the ring; the which I did deny him
And suffer'd him to go displeased away;
Even he that did uphold the very life
Of my dear friend. What should I say, sweet lady?
I was enforced to send it after him;
I was beset with shame and courtesy;
My honour would not let ingratitude
So much besmear it. Pardon me, good lady;
For, by these blessed candles of the night,
Had you been there, I think you would have begg'd
The ring of me to give the worthy doctor.

PORTIA

Let not that doctor e'er come near my house:
Since he hath got the jewel that I loved,
And that which you did swear to keep for me,
I will become as liberal as you;
I'll not deny him any thing I have,
No, not my body nor my husband's bed:
Know him I shall, I am well sure of it:
Lie not a night from home; watch me like Argus:

If you do not, if I be left alone,
Now, by mine honour, which is yet mine own,
I'll have that doctor for my bedfellow.
NERISSA
And I his clerk; therefore be well advised
How you do leave me to mine own protection.
GRATIANO
Well, do you so; let not me take him, then;
For if I do, I'll mar the young clerk's pen.
ANTONIO
I am the unhappy subject of these quarrels.
PORTIA
Sir, grieve not you; you are welcome notwithstanding.
BASSANIO
Portia, forgive me this enforced wrong;
And, in the hearing of these many friends,
I swear to thee, even by thine own fair eyes,
Wherein I see myself--
PORTIA
Mark you but that!
In both my eyes he doubly sees himself;
In each eye, one: swear by your double self,
And there's an oath of credit.
BASSANIO
Nay, but hear me:
Pardon this fault, and by my soul I swear
I never more will break an oath with thee.
ANTONIO
I once did lend my body for his wealth;
Which, but for him that had your husband's ring,
Had quite miscarried: I dare be bound again,
My soul upon the forfeit, that your lord
Will never more break faith advisedly.
PORTIA

Then you shall be his surety. Give him this
And bid him keep it better than the other.

ANTONIO

Here, Lord Bassanio; swear to keep this ring.

BASSANIO

By heaven, it is the same I gave the doctor!

PORTIA

I had it of him: pardon me, Bassanio;
For, by this ring, the doctor lay with me.

NERISSA

And pardon me, my gentle Gratiano;
For that same scrubbed boy, the doctor's clerk,
In lieu of this last night did lie with me.

GRATIANO

Why, this is like the mending of highways
In summer, where the ways are fair enough:
What, are we cuckolds ere we have deserved it?

PORTIA

Speak not so grossly. You are all amazed:
Here is a letter; read it at your leisure;
It comes from Padua, from Bellario:
There you shall find that Portia was the doctor,
Nerissa there her clerk: Lorenzo here
Shall witness I set forth as soon as you
And even but now return'd; I have not yet
Enter'd my house. Antonio, you are welcome;
And I have better news in store for you
Than you expect: unseal this letter soon;
There you shall find three of your argosies
Are richly come to harbour suddenly:
You shall not know by what strange accident
I chanced on this letter.

ANTONIO

I am dumb.

BASSANIO
> Were you the doctor and I knew you not?

GRATIANO
> Were you the clerk that is to make me cuckold?

NERISSA
> Ay, but the clerk that never means to do it,
> Unless he live until he be a man.

BASSANIO
> Sweet doctor, you shall be my bed-fellow:
> When I am absent, then lie with my wife.

ANTONIO
> Sweet lady, you have given me life and living;
> For here I read for certain that my ships
> Are safely come to road.

PORTIA
> How now, Lorenzo!
> My clerk hath some good comforts too for you.

NERISSA
> Ay, and I'll give them him without a fee.
> There do I give to you and Jessica,
> From the rich Jew, a special deed of gift,
> After his death, of all he dies possess'd of.

LORENZO
> Fair ladies, you drop manna in the way
> Of starved people.

PORTIA
> It is almost morning,
> And yet I am sure you are not satisfied
> Of these events at full. Let us go in;
> And charge us there upon inter'gatories,
> And we will answer all things faithfully.

GRATIANO
> Let it be so: the first inter'gatory
> That my Nerissa shall be sworn on is,

Whether till the next night she had rather stay,
Or go to bed now, being two hours to day:
But were the day come, I should wish it dark,
That I were couching with the doctor's clerk.
Well, while I live I'll fear no other thing
So sore as keeping safe Nerissa's ring.

Exeunt

Biography

A Short Life of Edward de Vere, 17th Earl of Oxford

by Dr. Kevin Gilvary, President
The de Vere Society

He was born on 12 April 1550 at Castle
Hedingham, his family's ancestral home. His father, John
de Vere, 16th Earl, was Lord Great Chamberlain and
attended the coronations of both Mary and Elizabeth
Tudor. His mother was Margaret Golding. Edward was 11
when, in 1561, Queen Elizabeth visited Hedingham for
four days of masques, feasting and entertainments. When
his father died in 1562, young Oxford left to become, like
Bertram in *All's Well that Ends Well*, a ward of the Crown
under the guardianship of William Cecil, the Queen's
private secretary (later Lord Burghley, Lord Treasurer).
His mother married Charles Tyrrell and seems to have
passed out of the boy's life. His sister Mary went to live
with her stepfather and the siblings were not reunited for
some years.

According to a curriculum in Cecil's own hand,
Edward de Vere's daily studies included dancing, French,
Latin, writing and drawing, cosmography, penmanship,
riding, shooting, exercise and prayer. Edward de Vere
showed a prodigious talent for scholarship from his early
years, and we may ascribe his lifelong love of learning to
the influence of two of his early tutors. The first was Sir
Thomas Smith who was, perhaps, England's most
respected Greek scholar and the former Cambridge tutor
of Sir William Cecil. It was, no doubt, through Cecil's

influence that Edward de Vere spent some time living in the household of Smith in his early years, during which time he spent about five months at Smith's alma mater, Queens' College, Cambridge. Smith was a scholar of widely varied interests – this was reflected in his 400-volume library, some of which is still extant at Cambridge. De Vere's other tutor was Laurence Nowell, who was not only an accomplished cartographer but was also England's premier scholar of Anglo-Saxon literature – it was Nowell who possessed the only known copy of *Beowulf*.

Another important influence on Edward de Vere's early studies was his maternal uncle Arthur Golding, an officer in the Court of Wards under Cecil, who is credited with the translation of Ovid's *Metamorphoses*, published in 1567, a book widely recognised as having a major influence on 'Shakespeare'.

Following on from his matriculation at Cambridge in November 1558, Edward was awarded an honorary MA by Cambridge during a Royal progress in August 1564, and another degree by Oxford University during a Royal progress in 1566. Edward de Vere then attended Gray's Inn to study law. One notable feature of the Elizabethan Inns of Court was a tradition of mounting dramatic productions and of hosting the various touring companies of players.

In 1570 he served in a military campaign in Scotland under the Earl of Sussex. By 1571, he was reported as a leading luminary of the Court and, for a time, a favourite of Queen Elizabeth. In December 1571 he married Anne Cecil, aged 15, daughter of his guardian. This was a dynastic marriage where all the advantage accrued to Cecil who, ennobled as Baron Burghley, had reduced the social gap between himself and the young Earl.

While Oxford was away on a Grand Tour of Europe, he heard that his daughter Elizabeth Vere had been born in July 1575. On his return in early 1576, he appeared to have been convinced that Elizabeth was not his child; consequently he became estranged from Anne for five years, and exiled himself from Court, taking up residence in the Savoy and concerning himself with literary and musical patronage.

Already, in 1573, *Cardanus Comfort* (the Consolations of Boethius) had been translated from Latin by Thomas Bedingfield and dedicated to Oxford; and published with a preface written by him. In 1576 an anthology, *A Paradise of Daintie Devices*, including several poems by Oxford, was published. These are juvenile works but already show affinities, in both style and thought, with those of the mature Shakespeare.

Oxford's Grand Tour had taken in Paris, Strasbourg, Venice, Genoa, Florence, Palermo and, on his way back through France, Rousillon – the setting for *Love's Labour's Lost*. Oxford spent the best part of a year travelling in Italy in 1576, and becoming involved with moneylenders. He came back to England fluent in Italian and well acquainted with the northern Italian cities, to be satirised by Gabriel Harvey as 'The Italian Earl'. On his way back his ship was attacked by pirates in the English Channel (cf. *Hamlet*). Fourteen of 'Shakespeare's' plays have Italian settings, in which he put his detailed knowledge of the country, beyond pure book knowledge, to good use.

1573 saw the birth of Henry Wriothesley, Earl of Southampton. Although history has not bequeathed to us any evidence of a direct relationship between the two men, in the relatively small world of the royal Court, they must have been acquainted with each other. The poems *Venus and Adonis* (1593) and *The Rape of Lucrece* (1594) were dedicated to Southampton. These were the first works to be published under the name 'Shakespeare' and for the next five years the records show the byline 'Shakespeare' to have been associated exclusively with these two poems. Plays under the name 'Shakespeare' did not appear in print until 1598, the year that Lord Burghley died.

In May 1577 Oxford invested in Frobisher's voyage in the ship *Edward Bonaventure*. Despite its name, the ship's voyage across the Atlantic in search of the North-West Passage lost money; consequently he was forced to sell three estates (cf. Hamlet's words 'I am but mad north-north-west' II.1.). In 1578 he invested in Frobisher's second expedition, which also lost money, forcing further sales of estates.

He was mentioned by Gabriel Harvey in an address to Queen Elizabeth in July 1578, as a prolific private poet and one 'whose countenance shakes spears'. In the same year John Lyly, Oxford's secretary, published *Euphues.The Anatomy of Wit*, followed in 1579 by *Euphues and his England*, dedicated to Oxford. These two books launched the fashion for 'Euphuism', a style characterized by high-flown language, satirized in *Love's Labour's Lost*.

In March 1581 Oxford's mistress, Anne Vavasour, who was one of Queen Elizabeth's Ladies of the Bedchamber, gave birth to a son. The lovers and their son were sent to the Tower by an infuriated Queen but swiftly released (cf. *Measure for Measure*). After his release, Oxford was wounded in a street-fight provoked by Thomas Knyvet, a kinsman of Anne Vavasour; affrays continued in the streets of London between the rival gangs of supporters for over a year (cf.*Romeo and Juliet*).

In December 1581 he resumed living with his long-suffering and devoted wife, and accepted Elizabeth

Vere as his child. Tragically, their only son died one day after his birth. Three more daughters followed, of whom Susan and Bridget survived.

In 1584, Robert Greene's *Gwydonius; the Card of Fancy* was dedicated to him, identifying him as a 'pre-eminent writer'. In 1586, when he was 36, he served on the tribunal which condemned Mary, Queen of Scots to execution.

In the same year, the Queen awarded Oxford an unconditional pension of £1,000 a year for life (about £500,000 at today's value). The motive for this uncharacteristic generosity on the part of the Queen remains a mystery – no accounting was required of Oxford. Her successor, King James I, continued to pay the pension. In reply to Sir Robert Cecil's request that Lord Sheffield's pension be increased, the King refused, saying, 'Great Oxford got no more . . .', leaving us to wonder why Great Oxford? His greatness does not seem to have resided in war or any of the known offices of State. Perhaps a clue can be found in a letter to Burghley, written in 1594, in which Edward de Vere seeks his favour in a matter involving what he describes as 'in mine office' and that this office is beholden to the Queen.

In 1589, George Puttenham published *The Arte of English Poesie* and this contains the most telling recognition of Edward de Vere's literary standing amongst his contemporaries: 'And in her Majesties time that now is are sprong up an other crew of Courtly makers Noble men and Gentlemen of her Majesties owne servantes, who have written excellently well as it would appeare if their doings could be found out and made publicke with the rest, of which number is first that noble Gentleman Edward Earle of Oxford.'

In 1588 his wife Anne, daughter of Lord Burghley, died and in extant letters written at this time, it is reported that Burghley is so incapacitated by grief over the death of his favourite daughter that he is incapable of conducting any Privy Council business.

Three years later, in 1591, Oxford married another of the Queen's Maids of Honour, Elizabeth Trentham, with whom he finally became the father of a male heir; Henry de Vere, 18th Earl of Oxford. Although there is evidence of his continued involvement in Court affairs, from the date of this marriage Edward de Vere's life at his new home at King's Place in Hackney is perhaps the most obscure of his entire life.

In 1594, his ship the *Edward Bonaventure* was wrecked in Bermuda (cf. *The Tempest*). In January 1595, Elizabeth Vere married William Stanley, 6th Earl of Derby, another literary earl who maintained his own company of players – many scholars believe that *A Midsummer Night's Dream* was written for these festivities which were attended by the whole royal Court.

On September 7 1598, Francis Meres' *Palladis Tamia* was registered for publication, naming Oxford as the 'best for comedy'. This is a vital document in Shakespearean history because it includes the first mention of 'Shakespeare' as a playwright, attributing twelve plays to him; until then Shakespeare's reputation had rested on the two narrative poems only.

Oxford suffered all his life from financial difficulties, much of which can be traced to the fact that Queen Elizabeth handed out the bulk of his estate to her favourite courtier the Earl of Leicester during Oxford's minority as a royal ward (estates which Oxford found almost impossible to reclaim), and the ruinous debt she placed upon him over his marriage to Anne Cecil. It is, however, notable that his new brother-in-law, the wealthy Staffordshire landowner and Knight of the Shire Francis Trentham, took over the management of Edward de

Vere's near-bankrupt estate from 1591 and gradually nursed it back to health so that, when Oxford died, all of his massive debts had been cleared.

On the Queen's death in 1603 Oxford wrote eloquently to Sir Robert Cecil, son and heir of Lord Burghley, of his 'great grief'. He wrote, 'In this common shipwreck, mine is above all the rest, who least regarded, though often comforted, she hath left to try my fortune among the alterations of time and chance'.

Oxford died in Hackney in 1604, cause unknown. Parish records state that he was buried in Hackney Church on July 6, but a family history by his first cousin Percival Golding, states 'Edward de Veer ... a man in mind and body absolutely accomplished with honorable endowments ... lieth buried at Westminster'. No record of such a burial can now be traced in Westminster Abbey, where there is a Vere family tomb.

The Aftermath of Oxford's life and death

During the winter season 1604-05, six of Shakespeare's plays were presented at Court by command of King James I. This has an air of commemoration. In 1609 the *Sonnets* were published in a pirated edition. The famous dedication describes the author as 'our ever-living', a phrase invariably used only of the dead.

In 1622 Henry Peacham published, in *The Compleat Gentelman*, a list of poets who made Elizabeth's reign a 'golden age'. Unaccountably, he omitted Shakespeare but placed the Earl of Oxford in first place in his list – perhaps he knew them to be the same person. This is unlike Meres who included them both – maybe one reason was because he didn't know Oxford and Shakespeare were the same person.

We do not know who instigated publication of the First Folio Edition of the Shakespeare plays in 1623, but there is no mention of any executor or relative of Shakspere of Stratford in connection with it. However, of the two brothers who financed it and to whom it was dedicated, one – Philip Earl of Montgomery – was the husband of Oxford's daughter Susan, while the other – William Earl of Pembroke – had once been a suitor for her sister Bridget. Pembroke was Lord Chamberlain, the supreme authority in the world of theatre, and thus in a position to decide which plays were to be published and which suppressed. We also know that Ben Jonson, who wrote much of the introductory material, was an intimate associate of the de Vere family after Oxford's death. The First Folio was therefore very much a family affair, but the family was not the one in Stratford-on-Avon.

An AfterVerse

For those with yet an interest
In strenuous debate
We've compiled a list of books and films
Your appetite to sate.
From this study clear your mind
Of doubt and all misgiving-
Who from us has long since gone
And who is ever-living.

Selected References & Bibliography
About the Author
Edward de Vere, 17th Earl of Oxford

Books

♦ Anderson, M. (2005). *Shakespeare by Another Name: The Life of Edward de Vere, Earl of Oxford, The Man who was Shakespeare.* New York: Gotham Books. *--A physicist by training with research interest in how evidence supports or negates a theory, Mark Anderson spent ten years investigating Edward de Vere as the author of Shake-speare's works.*

♦Farina, William. (2006). *De Vere as Shakespeare: An Oxfordian Reading of the Canon.* Jefferson, NC. McFarland & Company.

--Each of the plays and poems is individually assessed and explored in its own chapter, using the innumerable connections between the text itself and the life of its author, Edward de Vere.

♦ Looney, J. Thomas (2018). *Shakespeare Identified.* Cary, N.C. Veritas Publicaations.
--First published in 1920 this book began the modern Oxfordian movement. From reading it, Sigmund Freud became convinced and John Galsworthy called it "the best detective story I ever read."

♦ Ogburn, C. (1992). *The Mysterious William Shakespeare.* McLean (Va.): EPM.
--An in depth exploration and must read foundational book on the authorship question.

♦Sobran, Joseph. (1997). *Alias Shakespeare: Solving the Greatest Literary Mystery of All Time.*
New York; The Free Press, A Division of Simon & Schuster.
--A concise exploration of the puzzling questions surrounding the authorship controversy with the evidence decisively supporting the case for Edward de Vere, the 17th Earl of Oxford, as the rightful author of the Shakespeare plays and poems.

♦Whittemore, Hank. (2016), *100 Reasons Shake-speare Was the Earl of Oxford.*
Somerville MA. Forever Press.
►Also with further discussion and public comment at: *Hank Whittemore's Shakespeare Blog.*
        https://hankwhittemore.com/
--In both the book and online blog cited above, Whittemore presents a concise introduction to the

authorship question that examines 100 different aspects, from biographical and historical records, that point to Edward de Vere as the true writer of the Shake-speare plays and poems.

Websites & Videos

▶ De Vere Society. (2019). The de Vere Society – Dedicated to the proposition that the works of Shakespeare were written by Edward de Vere, 17th Earl of Oxford. [online] Deveresociety.co.uk. Available at: https://deveresociety.co.uk
--A very complete resource with substantial biographical and authorship information and links.

▶ The Oxford Fellowship (2019). Shakespeare Oxford Fellowship | Research and Discussion of the Shakespeare Authorship Question. [online] Shakespeare Oxford Fellowship. Available at: https://shakespeareoxfordfellowship.org/
--A seminal online resource especially focusing on the authorship question.

▶ Waugh, A. (2019). Alexander Waugh. [online] YouTube. Available at: https://www.youtube.com/channel/UCHN7SCKlsa9lPYJ mqqQ2uIg/featured/
OR simply search: 'Alexander Waugh'
--Alexander Waugh is a leading authorship scholar who has produced many fascinating video presentations on the authorship question. This link is to his YouTube Channel.

► Columbia Pictures & Centropolis Entertainment. (2011). *Anonymous.* Produced and directed by Roland Emmerich. [DVD]

--This mainstream film is both entertaining and enlightening. It presents a superb dramatization of the character of Edward de Vere, setting out in detail the historical and personal context which made his anonymous authorship necessary.

►Centropolis Entertainment and First Folio Pictures. *Last Will and Testament.* (2012). [DVD]

--A thoughtful and ground-breaking video documentary introduction to the Shakespeare authorship question.

Acknowledgment
Our sincere thanks to
The de Vere Society
and
The Shakespeare Oxford Fellowship
*for their inspiration, help and support
in creating this series.*

Attributions
*--Character list from Wikipedia under
the Creative Commons License 3.0
--Play text from the Moby(tm) editions
in the public domain*

Photos

Coat of Arms of Edward de Vere
Source: Wikimedia.org
Author: George Baker / Public domain

The Keep at Castle Hedingham
Source: geograph.org.uk
Author: David Phillips / CC BY-SA 2.0

The de Vere Family Coat of Arms
Source: Wikimedia
Author: Rs-nourse / CC BY-SA 3.0
(https://creativecommons.org/licenses/by-sa/3.0)

View from The Minstrels' Gallery, Hedingham Castle
Source: geograph.org.uk/p/3162585
Photo by: © PAUL FARMER - cc-by-sa/2.0

Cover inset: With thanks to rachid Er-ratibe at Pexels.com

Cover/Inside: The Welbeck portrait of Edward de Vere (1575).
Artist unknown. National Portrait Gallery, London.

This work has been edited and produced by

Verus Publishing
www.verusbooks.com

Ⅴ | Ρ

www.ingramcontent.com/pod-product-compliance
Lightning Source LLC
Chambersburg PA
CBHW030420100426
42812CB00028B/3039/J